Legacy of Evil

By Tommy Cox

Table of Contents

Preface

This manuscript, "LEGACY OF EVIL", was written by Thomas Cox in 1987 while in Mecklenburg prison.

Tommy was born on June 17th 1947 in Norfolk Virginia to a loving mother and a neglectful, angry father. His only sister died in adolescence and his mother died when Tommy was sixteen, leaving him with a father who was never present.

When Tommy was 19 he was incarcerated in a state work gang facility where he stayed for 10 years. After being out of prison for about a year Tommy was back in the system, this time a state prison where he quickly learned how to survive. He was looked upon as a leader and had many of followers.

Because of his role as a leader he was transferred to a prison in New Mexico to separate him from his followers. New Mexico was chosen because the prisoners there hated blacks and it was hoped that he would be killed by fellow prisoners. When that didn't happen, he was moved to a prison in Connecticut. With improved surroundings he studied for a paralegal degree and became a Christian.

Upon release he became a strong, caring defender of black youths and continued on his path of being a follower of Christ. He and his friend, Jo White, started the "Saving Our Youth" program in Richmond, Virginia and brought The Guardian Angels to that state capital.

This manuscript is dedicated to Tommy's loving daughter and grandchildren. Special thanks to Tommy's friends Walt Hitchcock and Suzanne Peterson for their help and support during the publishing of this manuscript.

Introduction

"It is not power that
corrupts but fear. Fear of
losing power corrupts those
who wield it, and fear of the
scourge of power corrupts those
who are subject to it."
      Aung San Suu Kyi, Nobel Peace Prize winner.

Mecklenburg Correctional Center, located in Boydton, Va., was a human warehouse for the rebellious, poor and powerless segment of Virginia. It was a "Frankenstein monster" created by stubborn old men with ancient ideas and values. After eight years of disaster, this monster finally began to turn against its vile creators with a ruinous vengeance. The violence and oppression there, so proficiently misled to the public by the news media, has been exposed to the world from a chronology of events which occurred within a nine month period. These events placed Mecklenburg prison under microscopic observation, and several investigations, even though they were inchoate, began to pierce the thick armor of the blatant lies that kept this monster alive and hungry for so long.

Residing at Mecklenburg as a prisoner was akin to experiencing the menacing horror of an unbeatable force, a raging force that brutalizes your mind, body and spirit. Our only shelter from this force was our "collective strength," and the southern, traditional fear of becoming broken men. Constantly in peril, our intellect and sense of humanity strangled, stumbling backwards in abjection, we fervently stood up as one and resorted to open warfare with the Mecklenburg regime. After eight years of self-destruction, this was a mode of recuperation for us; a recrudescence so illustrious that it affected Virginia prisoners in every institution throughout the state.

Mecklenburg authorities believed in reform or control through illogical punishment and programming prisoners to automation. In Virginia prisons the authorities were unparalleled in stifling the capacity of prisoners to examine their own problems and think for themselves. The concept of rehabilitation was just an illusion, and prisoners were being treated as "chattel slaves" who were required to practice total obedience or be subjected to the ferocious attacks of the mindless guards. Most Mecklenburg prisoners had a forlorn look; life consisted of only one violent event after another for the average prisoner incarcerated the

The repression at Mecklenburg prison had transcended mere prison problems. The racist and sick mentalities of the Mecklenburg rulers incisively agree with "American tradition." The mentality of the "heartless administrator" is equivalent to the mentalities of the Klansman, the imperialist, the super-rich capitalist, and the wagging tail Negros who so faithfully follow them. These type mentalities established America's present power, and today are swaying the World's adjuration of her. Believe me, these people revel in other people's misery.

February 10, 1984 it was revealed that Mecklenburg officials had sanctioned the tapping of death row prisoners' phone calls to lawyers from December 18th to January 21. They made efforts to justify this by stating that their "illegal actions" were essential in preventing another humiliating death row escape. They claimed to have received information from an informant of another death row escape in process. This was just another facet of the many illegal and unjust tactics of the Mecklenburg officials who controlled this "tomb of horrors" with an unhindered leeway to tyranny.

Legitimate attempts by prisoners to voice their opposition to this "Fresh Alcatraz" were rebuffed at every door. The governor and other Virginia politicians showed a kind of malignant neglect towards them. With nowhere to turn, pressed into desperation, many Mecklenburg prisoners became irrational from this mental state of hopelessness. Subsequently the actions from this irrationality were broadcasted to the public. The American public has a reputation for passing judgment from the concept of any establishment propaganda.

There is always more than one side to an issue. Prison administrators enjoy an unremitting access to the media and their propaganda is blessed with an infectious quality. The prisoners have no vehicle of exposure, and with relentless society has become unsympathetic does not conform to any method crime waves sweeping the country, towards them. But this attitude of reasoning because this was a major "social problem" with human animals being manufactured within its belly; animals who'd one day be released to unleash their inner, prison induced hatred upon innocent members of society.

Mecklenburg prison was Virginia's first "experimental control
unit." There has always been segregation units which were designed to keep prisoners locked up for violating the prisons' rules. The prisoner could be put in the hole or placed in "administrative segregation." If the prisoner received no additional write ups, he could get out of the hole in 30 days or less; he could get out of administrative segregation within a year.

Control units were established for the total control of the so called unmanageable prisoners, and their objectives were not to just secure or punish prisoners for prison infractions. They were designed to crush the prisoners, psychologically and physically. No matter what the prisoner's offense was he could be in a control unit until the completion of his original prison sentence. Control units more depraved than Mecklenburg prison are turning men into vegetables and unstable animals across this country today.

B.F. Skinner, a so called behavior expert, created the "behavior modification" techniques which are used in all control units. This technique is the infamous "carrot or stick" approach. This technique was also predominant in the federal control unit at Marion, Illinois.

Based on my experience and understanding, I have a lot to say about prisons and how they ultimately affect today's societies. I feel it's vital at this dismal period for enlightening "prison literature" to reach the minds of the America people. They should be allowed to judge the merits of these type projects.

There has been a considerable body of critical work produced on the United States prison system, but this by no means should cause any American to suggest that there's nothing left to say on this subject. "Legacy of Evil" is my attempt to contribute to people's understanding of just what goes on in these imperialist hellholes... and what that signifies about the nature of this system and the people who continues to rule it. The simple fact is, our whole criminal justice system is in disrepair. It's antiquated, overloaded and operates to corrupt rather than rehabilitate the offender consigned to it. I think this system has become an affront to the entire American public.

The Legacy Of Evil is about more than American prisons; it's about the responsibilities of the American people and the politicians whom they elect in trust; it's about the willingness, without fear of consequences, to criticize capitalism and classism; an appeal to the American .conscience: for a deeper analysis of why so few have so much while so many have so little. The Legacy of Evil is also a voice for the thousands of inconspicuous men and women who've spent most of their floundering lives in and out of American prisons, feeling powerless to influence what goes on outside the walls. They will understand; their reality is my reality.

In the Legacy Of Evil I will strive to bring to life the appalling and bizarre world of Mecklenburg prison, a world of "totalitarian methodology," where ingenious death row prisoners organized the most momentous death row escape in American history, where gruesome punishment was Inflicted on prisoners unabatedly, where bodily waste, urine and stale food permeated the atmosphere of every building, where revolt after revolt occurred and grown men sank to animalistic levels of survival.

Here is a chronology of 1984 and 1985 events in connection with Mecklenburg .prison:

April and May Prison officials receive tips that a breakout on death row is planned. Extensive searches are launched.

May 31- The largest death row escape in the history of this country occurs. The escapees, accused and convicted of murdering ten people, were brothers Linwood and James Briley, Derick Peterson, Willie Jones, Earl Clanton Jr., and Lem Tuggle.

June 1- The convicts' escape vehicle, a Mecklenburg prison van, is found in Warrenton County, North Carolina; the fugitives abduct a motorist in Warrenton, North Carolina. Clanton and Peterson are recaptured without a struggle in Warrenton.

June 2- Robert M. Landon, Director of the Virginia Department of Corrections, stated that a breakdown in human engineering enabled the six convicts to escape, but that warden Gary L. Bass properly handled tips that an escape plot was being hatched on death row.

June 4- Sixteen Mecklenburg employees, including 14 hostages, a tower guard and van driver, are put on administrative leave until the end of the investigation. An American Civil Liberties Union Lawyer in Washington, D. C., blames the death row escape on the department's administration, which he said failed to provide adequate training for the guards.

June 5- Governor Charles S. Rob announces that a three person team of corrections experts from outside of Virginia will begin an independent investigation of the death row escape.

June 7- Lem Tuggle and Willie Jones are captured in Vermont; Jones gave himself up after a phone conversation with his mother.

June 11- Officials in North Carolina close the Warren County command post and concede that the Brileys are not in their state.

June 19- The Brileys are captured without any resistance in Philadelphia.

June 22- Warden Bass and two other top officials at the prison are removed from the Mecklenburg regime and assigned duties elsewhere.

June 23- State officials reveal that the escapees had hidden homemade knives in wall cracks which they had painted over, easily eluding detection during frequent shakedowns.

July 5- Five guards are fired; Bass and Deputy Warden Harold Catron are suspended for ten days without pay.

July 12- Nine guards and six convicts are injured in a 75 minute disturbance.

July 25- Acting warden Sherman L. Townley restricts prison visits by non-relatives of the prisoners_

July 26- Mecklenburg prisoners experienced random brutality by prison officials from other institutions in the process of a major shakedown, presumably to foil hostage taking.

July 29- Officials reveal that another breakout effort was foiled when guards, during a random search, found that window struts had been cut out.

August 4- Convicts armed with handmade knives take eight guards and one female kitchen worker hostage. Two badly wounded guards are released.

August 5-   A letter I sent to the Richmond Times Dispatch, denouncing the illegal treatment of Mecklenburg prisoners, was published.

October 12- Linwood Briley is executed in the Virginia's electric chair at 11 p.m.

April 18, 1985- Nine prison guards were seriously stabbed by convicts at the state penitentiary in Richmond, Va. Later that night, James Briley, after eating a last meal of fried shrimp and a soft drink, was executed at 11:02 p.m. He was pronounced dead at 11:07 p.m.

August 21- I was exiled from the Virginia prison system, for political reasons, to the state prison system of Santa Fe, New Mexico.

Convicts versus Inmates

There is a great contrast between convicts and inmates in the Virginia prisons. This may seem trivial and foolish to outsiders, and it may be difficult to comprehend, but it is a titanic problem, and it has become the most powerful catalyst in aggravating the tumultuous settings of Virginia institutions. This deadly conflict is never relaxed, and the unyielding hatred between the two is evident in nearly every aspect of prison life.

Historically, this conflict has been perpetual in Virginia prisons, but years earlier ʻthe administration refused to openly acknowledge its existence. Convict was the official label for all prisoners. The label inmate did not surface until recent years after the psychological mind games came into effect.

Initially, brute force was the only solution to all prison problems. There were horrible activities in which the prisoners were forced to contend with: solitary confinement with no set time limitations, distressful living conditions, starvation diets in solitary, which consisted of bread and water twice a day and a full meal once every third day. These were disquieting experiences for any human being to undergo, but the most critical activities were the daily tear gassings, beatings, and occasional murders inflicted upon them by prison guards. These obnoxious activities created the convict and destroyed the spirit and souls of some enough to create the inmate.

The convicts and inmates were both chattel but only the inmate accepted and succumbed to this. The social phenomenon that engaged the consciousness of convicts was rebellion, whereas acquiescence engaged the consciousness of inmates. Deplorable conditions will either summon inner strength to enable individuals to endure, or break them down completely and suck them into the web of a consuming weakness which introduces self-hatred. Degradation upon degradation is capable of burning out the human qualities of weak people and instilling in them crude cretins.

Inmates became indispensable to the prison administration because they allowed their will to be broken. They had no alternative but to run to prison officials and turn informers, volunteer for jobs which convicts considered demeaning, and grin and scratch their funky behinds all day like the little weasels that they are.

. The prison regime used these half-men to disrupt any efforts of organized protest, to foil escapes, etc. They were rewarded with early parole, better jobs, a pat on the back far serious infractions, and genuine smiles from their guard protectors. They walked the yard with prison guards, laughing, joking, and addressing them by their first names. Inevitably, the labels inmate and guard were being applied interchangeably in Virginia prisons.

No convict would reveal any secret to an inmate for fear of it reaching the ears of prison officials. The inmates clung to each other because they felt that convicts were inexorably scheming to harm them. Convicts and inmates became super-paranoid of each other. This tradition still lingers today.

Prisoners entering Virginia prisons quickly decide their status among other prisoners. After they've decided, they then .will know who and who not to associate with. Birds of the same feather really do flock together in Virginia prisons.

During the hundreds of years that black Africans were chattel slaves, there were two diverse categories of slaves which the slave masters easily recognized: field and house slaves. The field slaves were an insolent let. They hated the slave master and did not adhere to his laws, because they considered them unjust and inhumane. They were spirited and imaginative, and their courage was continually regenerated with the belief in the righteousness of their convictions. They rebelled, committed sabotage, escaped, and even murdered slave masters from the anger and frustration of their painful predicament. The house slaves were just the opposite. They were humble, obedient and fearful; but they also were shrewd and ambivalent. It was never a guarantee that they would not aid the field slave. Even so, they appeared

to love the slave master and his family. They nurtured his

children, informed on the field slave whenever there was

an escape plot or conspiracy to harm him, prepared the

food for his family, and even sincerely wept when there

was death in his family.

Convicts and Inmates, in this regard, have acquired an

identical connection with their oppressors. Inmates appear

to love prison officials, while convicts expose their

contempt for them in variation. Inmates are in the

majority and they have attained a certain degree of power

within the prison system in exchange for their manhood

and self-respect.

The same diabolical methods that were used against

African slaves to create fear and low self-esteem are being

used against Virginia prisoners today. This system's

objective is to produce as many inmates as possible.

African slaves were stripped of their original names,

language, culture and dignity. They were divided from

their loved ones and encouraged emphatically against

unity. The weaker slaves, who did not possess the fortitude

to endure the process of dehumanization, lost themselves completely and begin to admire and praise the oppressor. Psychologically, their immense self-hatred increased their devotion to the oppressor because they saw in him what they were brainwashed to believe were superior qualities. The oppressor had conquered them, he ordered them about with no questions asked, he taught and fed them, and even took pleasure from involuntary sex with them without fear or threat of receiving criminal Charges. He became, in their minds, unequivocally their lord and master. Weak people have a tendency to worship their lord and master.

When a prisoner enters the Virginia prison system, the authorities give him a number and his name becomes almost non-existent. They immediately began the procedure of mind control. He is programmed to obey orders and to allow the administration to do his thinking for him. Neither rehabilitation nor any facet of it is mentioned, because this system is just not designed to focus its attention upon rehabilitating anyone.

The prison guard adopts the role of lord and master. He enforces the laughable regulations, while strutting around the prison compound with his precious stun gun; he can send any prisoner to solitary with trumped up charges, and he asserts his power over the prisoners on a daily basis. After losing their names and sense of self, submissive prisoners become totally dependent upon the prison guards. At times I have watched them gazing at the guards in their crisp uniforms with the lecherous look of a passionate female. The guards sense this admiration and quickly use this to their advantage. It has never been a difficult task in distinguishing inmates from any other type prisoner within this system.

One of the most obvious traits of a convict is his inability to fully adjust to daily prison life. It is an abnormal environment with abnormal rules and behavior to him. He may not be well educated or highly political, but common sense tells him that he has to resist everything the authorities are attempting to do to him. Pride, and a belief in universal rights, initiates substance to the convict. This can become akin to spirituality in its strength and intriguing nature. A convict, whether he is apolitical or political, educated or uneducated, angry or calm, will strive to be treated as a human being under any circumstance. Nothing upon this earth, short of death, can obliterate this longing from him. Regardless of the nature of their crimes, convicts who're standing on principles will demand respect!

There will always be revolts and resistance within America's prisons because prison authorities refuse to accept this natural characteristic that will be infinitely dominate in the strong minded male and female. Humans cannot be treated like animals without dire consequences.

The inmate blends in the prison system like a grasshopper blends in grass. He is ideal for effective prison control, but these feeble creatures are detrimental to society and themselves because their mental weaknesses render them less capable of elevating themselves to higher levels of Life. Mental strength and incentive are the ingredients that transform prisoners into changed and responsible individuals. Most inmates are hopeless cases who will gleefully remain criminals throughout their lives. They even lack the capacity to truthfully care for others because they have conscientiously dismissed the love of self. The love of self is a law of nature which should never be deleted, because without it we lose a basic quality that makes us more human. Ninety per cent of the drug addicts and alcoholics in this country have injured the hunger for this law of nature.

Convicts are the most zealous in eradicating their prior deficiencies. They develop their minds from a principal need to be equal or above the oppressor in intelligence and character. They are convinced that prison officials are criminals to a higher degree than they are, and that they avoid prosecution and suspicions through their status in the eyes of American society. Prison officials conveniently argue that prisoners have committed crimes against society and that attention should not be geared so much towards rehabilitation. They convey the concept that developing the minds and characters of prisoners is not near as important as ware housing them and keeping them off the streets. Most of them feel that punishment is the supreme retribution for their crimes. If all prisoners were incorrigible idiots who commit crimes just for the thrill of it, then this concept would be reasonable. Esteemed criminologists can confirm that this is not the case at all. American societies are not faultless, even though they are not entirely to blame. The motives causing the acts that have placed so many people in American prisons are meaningful enough to dwell into.

A grand percentage of prisoners are black and lived way below the poverty level in the streets. There is, as it has been, incessant racism, discrimination, unemployment, police brutality, poor housing, etc., in this country. Poor people react to these situations in dissimilar fashions, but reality tells us that all poor people will not capitulate to docility, and there will remain manifestations of opposition in a country ruled by a handful of wealthy people. There is no demonstrative display of significant support or sentiment from the government towards the improvidence of poor Americans, especially black Americans.

Most convicts first enter prison plagued with inchoate mentalities, but after they have been voluntarily incorporated into the process of introspection and study, they begin to lucidly understand what is happening to people like them in America. This new found awareness designs the psychic trauma that forms added resentment. Awareness makes the convicts more unmanageable. Ignorant prisoners are more susceptible to lies and tricks.

Convicts eventually see themselves as victims, and many of them will attempt to reform themselves as a statement of revenge against prison authorities. If prison authorities propose that it is inconceivable that convicts are capable of positive change, then they will attempt to change positively just to prove them wrong. The convicts and the prison officials embrace the "them against us" philosophy, and this is evident throughout the Virginia prison system.

I am not suggesting here that there should be crime in this nation without punishment, but: I am saying that human beings are not born criminals. A vast number of people convicted of crimes are indoctrinated by the rapidly deteriorating moral fiber of American society.

Yet society endorses the final mental destruction of these people by today's standards of prison policies.

Convicts are aware of this grave situation, and they are concerned with their mistreatment in prison just as people are concerned with their mistreatment on the outside. They realize that many of them are criminals because of extenuating circumstances.

Inmates are "Lost souls" who are not interested in any factor that would upgrade their Lives. They have no ethics or morals, and they are erratic. Many of these prisoners are rapists, child molesters; predators of physically weaker people. The Virginia penal system is releasing this caliber of prisoner earlier than most. These buffoons are given parole and allowed to stalk freely among the people in various communities in Virginia. These prisoners have become a thorn in everyone's side excluding prison officials; they also were an asset to the emotionless administration that produced and precipitated the bloody eruptions that rocked the Mecklenburg prison to its core!

Beginning

"Abandon all hope

You who enter here"

Dante's Inferno

Mecklenburg prison officially opened in the spring of 1977. Rumors about its modern structure and unorthodox rules were surging throughout the Virginia prison system with unquenchable intensity.

At this period I was confined to C-Building, a maximum security building within the walls of the State Penitentiary. C-Building is a diminutive structure of bricks and steel which holds 72 prisoners in the upper portion of the building and 28 in the downstairs isolation section. This building is actually a "prison within a prison" for troublesome prisoners who've violated prison rules such as disobeying a direct order, being in a restricted area, fighting another prisoner, etc.

The convict or inmate (the odds are always in favor of it being a convict) who's suspected of violating one or more of these rules is removed from the main population and sent to C-Building, placed in a regular cell upstairs until his scheduled appearance before the Adjustment Committee, a small group of prison employees. If the prisoner is convicted by the Adjustment Committee, he can receive 15 days in isolation (the maximum) on each charge, a suspended sentence, or a verbal reprimand.

There is a large steel door in front of the bars of each isolation cell. This door has a port hole approximately six inches from the top which can be closed at any time by the guards. Isolated prisoners are denied access to any personal property excluding items for hygiene, and desert is omitted from their meals. If the charge was not major the prisoner is returned to main population after the conclusion of the sentence. If it was major he would be urged to appear before the I.C.C. (Institutional Classification Committee) for a higher degree of security, which could be 90 days upstairs or a transfer to another maximum security institution.

Prior to the opening of Mecklenburg, C-Building at the State Penitentiary and M-Building at the Powhatan Correctional Center, were the only two maximum security buildings in the state designed to hold hardened prisoners. Convicts were shifted from C-Building to M-Building in a vicious cycle, sometimes remaining in these filthy, roach infested cells for years.

The much awaited opening of Mecklenburg prison was a spectacular event for prison officials. They were ecstatic as they boldly strutted the tiers of the State Pen boasting about their new "super prison." Revelations of what the Mecklenburg rulers pledged evoked memories of the good old days and esoteric smiles were etched on their faces. They felt that they had lost control of certain situations from the results of a major riot in December of 1972. Positive innovations for the prisoners at the State Pen had come into effect, and most of the diehard officials who believed in the old methods were visibly upset with this. They were anxiously anticipating the opening of Mecklenburg prison because it promised to give them the edge: tighter security, larger stun guns, and more freedom to create and brutalize a disorderly environment.

It was no accident or coincident that most of the guards who were influenced by these perverted values were the first to be hired at Mecklenburg prison. Many of them became ranking officers at Mecklenburg in a relatively short period.

The possibility of being transferred to Mecklenburg didn't faze me. I had been incarcerated since 1969, and had survived atrocious ordeals on numerous slave camps (road camps) prior to my arrival at the State Pen. I was now renowned throughout the system for fervently struggling against the institutionalized racism and barbarity of Virginia's prison system. Mecklenburg prison was just another dungeon (in a different location) to me. I didn't think that it was possible for Virginia officials to devise an institution which would exceed the others in unsatisfactory and indecent conditions.

I had been transferred to C-Building from M-Building for allegedly stabbing another prisoner in the population of the Powhatan Correctional Center. The charge had been dismissed and the I.C.C. had informed me that they were pondering the possibility of releasing me to the population of the State Pen. But this was all prior to the opening of Mecklenburg prison, the new "concentration camp" for the most uncooperative prisoners.

There were six of us designated to be the first prisoners of Mecklenburg prison. We were the unfortunate convicts that the prison regime wanted to see writhe first—in the gloomy atmosphere of the monster which, they had created. This little group consisted of me, Henry (Bobilly) Gorham, Leroy (Dog) Harris, Thomas (Top Cat) Pen, Leroy Boone, and Ike Rogers. Rogers was the only white prisoner among us.

We were escorted singly to the Penitentiary hospital and given thorough physical examinations. The next morning we were hauled into a blue van and transported to Mecklenburg prison.

Arriving at Mecklenburg two hours later, I was absolutely amazed while gazing at its outward appearance. It resembled a large, plush college campus. The complete area was sparkling clean with well-trimmed lawns and solid smooth pavements. A conglomerate of miniature trees, gun towers and barbed wire fences were dazzlingly exposed through the heated rays of the sun.

While sitting in this oven like van, sweating copiously, it suddenly occurred to me that naive visitors would be highly impressed by this radiant scenery. Most prisons apply this psychological game of beautiful facades to deceive gullible investigators, but this quickly became a consummate skill of Mecklenburg authorities. Nothing there was as it seemed to be.

When the back van door slid open, we all stared into the solemn faces of the Pert Team, a special group of guards whose sole purpose was force. Standing slightly ahead of them in all of his glory, was Harold Catron, Chief of security and former king of C-Building. Catron was a typical prison guard who rises rapidly in the hierarchy of the administration. There are few requirements: be brutal, display no remorse for your brutality, never submit to a prisoner under any circumstances, be able to read and write, and always remember that the prison rule book is your brains.

Catron was exceptionally cruel during his reign of C-Building. Placing a man of this disposition in such a prestigious status at a new and controversial prison convinced us that the dismal predictions of our future (from prison grapevine) were going to be correct. Just the sight of this man's unattractive face stirred poignant emotions in many Virginia prisoners.

In the basement of Building-I, we were in a huddle, impatiently enduring the malicious glares of the Pert Team. Joining Catron was Lt. Henry, another racist official, who was a former member of the lunatic fringe that controlled C-Building.

Catron stared fiercely at us and said coldly, "Well, jive mother fuckers, you're in my fuckin hands now. This is a brand new ball game. You will be made believers this time. Now take off those god damn clothes!"

We were lost in our own thoughts as we stripped, steeling ourselves for the inevitable harassment and humiliation. Lt. Henry beckoned me to a long table where my personal belongings were.

"You will have to buy new stuff," he informed me. "Even the cosmetics and personal clothing will have to be replaced. Nothing here stays but what's on this list." He handed me a memo listing what we were allowed to keep.

"Man, are you crazy?" I asked him indignantly. "You pigs can't do this kinda shit!"

We glared at each other without moving.

"Be cool Tommy," I heard my comrades utter behind me. "Man, that's exactly what they want you to do."

The rest of this ritual was followed: through in silence. All of our personal property except legal papers, 10 personal letters, family photos and religious material, was packed to be shipped to whatever address we gave them. We were later issued two sets of state clothes, a towel, shower shoes, high top boots, socks, soap, toothpaste, toothbrush, two sheets, a pillowcase and blanket.

Flanked by the Pert Team, we were escorted upstairs to pod-A, an area which consisted of 12 cells; six to each two tiers. A shower stall was stationed at the end of each corridor. Operation of the cell doors was controlled electronically by a guard from a tiny glass enclosed control room, only inches from the entrance to the pod. There were eight pods to each building. The control room of each pod divides it into a left and right section, each with 12 cells and a day room in which prisoners can mingle at recreation periods.

Inside the cell I immediately noticed the few modern alterations: there was hot and cold water, a control knob for the back window, a circulation vent was located inches above the toilet, a mirror was implanted in the wall, and a large steel desk stood in the corner with sections for cosmetics, books, etc. This was the equivalent of a luxury hotel compared to the funky, primitive C-Building. There also were no bars! They were replaced by a sliding steel door with a narrow strip of sturdy glass approximately 30 inches long and four inches wide.

That evening an institutional memo was slipped under the door of my cell. I stood in the middle of the floor and began reading it. Half way through it I was seething with rage, and my legs no longer felt strong enough to hold me up. It declared:

Welcome to Mecklenburg Correctional Center. This center, as you may know, was established as an institution for inmates who have proved to be violent and unmanageable at previous institutions, inmates who have committed serious infractions of rules, to the extent that they can no longer be properly maintained in a regular population environment.

Here it will be a necessity that you undergo a three phase progressive program. The phase program will allow you to obtain additional privileges as you move up in the phases. You can do this only by conducting yourselves as mature and responsible men and obeying institutional rules. The phase program can be completed in a ten month period, if you conduct yourselves properly. After the program is completed successfully you will be transferred back to a general population institution. You can extend your stay here by violating rules, and the only way you can leave here is to successfully complete the phase program.

The staff here will be responsive to your needs and complaints. No member of the staff will act capriciously or without regards to your needs. We will make every attempt to communicate our policies and expectations to you, but we will not tolerate any of your previous aggressiveness. We will meet force with force, and we will do what is necessary to protect our staff.

The memo was signed by Warden Gene Johnson, a beady eyed, pale faced drunkard of short stature, who adhered unequivocally to the tradition of guard force. He was by no means a liberal in prison tactics, but eventually Catron made him appear as one. He would be no match for the steadfast ambitions of Catron. In reality, Catron was running the show at Mecklenburg from the very beginning. With the force of his volatile personality and his numerous contacts, he quickly overpowered Johnson. The entire prison staff listened to his schismatic ideas and submitted to his power, even though it obviously was not in accord with his rank. He had his way without any opposition, yet his thirst for power and chaos was insatiable.

The next day the evil and provocative nature of the Mecklenburg staff was presented to us. In conformity to American standard, most prison authorities treat prisoners in an animalistic manner and diligently exert energy in encouraging the prisoners to think .of themselves as less than human. Gradually as prisoners began to think this way they began to act in agreement with their thoughts;

and it is much easier to pummel a human animal than a rational, helpless prisoner.

The control room guard had to crack our cell doors a few inches to enable us to receive food trays from the guards. Staring at the meager contents of the trays in disbelief, we began to shout complaints in unison. The guards laughed at us and walked away. The noon and evening meals were similar. Complaining vigorously during the serving of the evening meal, the noxious Pert Team gathered in front of our cells to show force; they were caressing huge stun guns (a temporarily paralyzing gun with a bean bag inside, which has a powerful impact). Any veteran prisoner would have recognized their facial expressions: they would rather brutalize us than make love to their wives or girlfriends at that particular moment.

There was very little discrepancy within our antagonized group. Oppression tends to bring people together, and they usually attempt to work with what they have regardless of the odds. It's a process that seems as natural as child birth.

After a week of the starvation diet, we discussed our predicament on the circulation vents and decided to declare a full hunger strike. Considering the deliberate rationing of the food, we agreed that a hunger strike could harbor no future horrors for us.

This was our first organized form of protest at Mecklenburg; this was a mentally and physically laborious effort from sound judgment, and the subsequent protests through the years were of unquestionable necessity. As conditions cumulated to an unbearable level, our protests and resistance naturally grew more profound. These are human conditions that are created wherever there are situations which consist of oppressors and the oppressed.

Regardless of the argument that we were indurate prisoners who deserved total control, we were still human beings capable of change. We reacted from ill treatment, but investigative documents will show that our initial protests were passive and less exciting than most Boy Scout complaints. Our protests elevated to higher stages because as President John F. Kennedy once stated: "Those who make peaceful revolution impossible will make violent evolution inevitable."

The Pert Team was beginning to evidence their Nazi-like mentality. We were not attacked physically but they perpetrated painful retaliation against us, mainly from childish taunts and threats of future mayhem. We were daily informed by them that the present situation would change as soon as Catron gave the word.

Physically and mentally exhausted after refusing food trays for three weeks, we were religiously pacing our cells, contemplating the appropriate strategy to pursue. These are always crucial moments in a prison setting because one instance of bad judgment can bring irretrievable harm and years of mentally—damaging regret.

The next morning I awoke to the fretful sounds of the Pert Team assembled in the day room of our .pod. Expecting the worse, I jumped out of bed, quickly dressed, wrapping a towel around my head for protection from club blows. Moments later I was gazing into the botched face of Warden Johnson. A few members of the Pert Team were standing closely behind him. He turned in the direction of the control room guard and demonstrated with his fingers how far he wanted my cell door cracked. The pod became deadly quiet except for the dull humming of the air conditioner. He attempted a false smile and I peered into his red eyes.

"Cox, listen to me because we want to start out right in this damn place," he spoke in a sluggish tone. "This institution just opened and there will be many little problems beyond our control. Now I understand the problems concerning the lack of food we are working on this and it should be rectified by the weekend or earlier; but you people are not going to bully us into doing a damn thing. I want this made crystal clear." Clearing his throat, he continued: "Following the same actions that brought you here in the first place will get you nowhere because it won't work here. This is the purpose of this place, to wean this arrogance and aggressiveness out of you. Come to us first when there's, a problem and give us a chance to work it out before you go into your gangster acts and force our hand. Behavior modification is relatively new in this state but I believe it can work if you give it a chance."

"Man, we are not a bunch of idiots," I said loudly. "We will do what we have to do here as we were forced to do at other institutions. We are well aware from previous experience the results of written letters and grievances to higher authorities. It's a waste of time. You are only trying to make us look like violent, brainless animals so you can dog us without any real feedback. We only ask to be treated as men. Everywhere we've been we've acted according to the way we were treated."

He sighed, and then said slowly, "Cox, you've got to act like a man in order to be treated like a man. I can't speak for those other places but as long as I am in control here, I assure you that you will not be mistreated unless you bring it on yourself. I must make you aware that your behavior is going to be the one most important factor considered in determining your treatment or length of stay here. It is my hope that each of you want very badly to get to a population environment. It is my hope and the hope of the staff; but you are the one that has to make that effort. It is senseless for you and the staff to continue your battles. I ask each of you to just stop and think for a minute before you act and act in a manner in which you would like to be treated. You may just get back what you put into it." He smiled, satisfied with the memory of his little speech.

"Yeah, alright man," I replied. I was bored with him and wanted him away from my cell. His con speech was void of any sincerity.

He asked me if I would continue the hunger strike, which I refused to answer, then to my relief, he moved on down the tier to Bobilly's cell. After talking to all six of us, we all agreed that the best thing he gave us was his departure from the pod.

Within three days the food was adequately prepared with a much higher quantity. We accepted our food trays and the atmosphere seemed less tensed, but we built no new expectations, and we knew this was an illusion because Catron was always in the background, watching and waiting.

About a week later I was writing a sentimental letter to my daughter and was interrupted by a great deal of commotion outside. I stepped to the back window and witnessed a number of prisoners from various Virginia institutions being hauled out of three prison vans; they were yelling and cursing while Mecklenburg guards barraged them with threats and insults. Catron was standing close to the first van with his meaty arms folded and a chilly smile on his face.

I recognized most of these cats, as they were rebels who had been in the Virginia prison system for many years. They were arbitrarily selected as candidates for Mecklenburg because the administration was eager to practice the principle of "behavior modification," and they wanted Mecklenburg to function immediately with a maximum population. Most of these convicts had only minor infractions on their records, but the only requirement to be a Mecklenburg prisoner was a major or minor record of violence or resistance.

After the newly arrived prisoners were processed, Building-1 and Building-2 were filled and the noise was deafening. Our pod had suddenly become a regular maximum security unit, with the usual foolish conversations and the childish and imbecilic actions, of adults to alleviate monotony. There was a well welcomed tranquility at two a.m. and we began to seek information concerning other comrades.

The opening of Mecklenburg prison had a tremendous impact upon every institution and just about every prisoner within the system. Swirling rumors had created Mecklenburg into the "Alcatraz" of Virginia. Sixty per cent of the prisoners would tremble just from the utterance of its name. Guards in other institutions controlled weaker prisoners with the constant threat of being sent to Mecklenburg. The tension and fear brought to existence from the opening of Mecklenburg was unavoidable. The monster was meeting the expectations of its creators.

Negative War

The Virginia Department of Corrections had embarked upon a disastrous form of behavioral engineering. They were attempting to modify the behavior of Mecklenburg prisoners who were acutely aware of their motives for offensively responding to unnecessary mistreatment. The officials at Mecklenburg knew that we were not ordinary prisoners clinging to individualism, and they were determined •to thwart any attempts to shape cohesive units that would pose a formidable threat to their control. Thus, the tactics they applied to avertedly stir our anger at crucial periods were customary tactics. They unceremoniously pitted prisoner against prisoner and isolated leaders and potential leaders from the more submissive prisoners. Even though we were at war with prison officials, personal conflicts with each other caused many of us to lose our perspectives.

Mecklenburg administrators, with all of their craftiness, cannot bear the full onus of the mindless war amongst ourselves. They added fuel to the violence of the war once its growth was cultivated, but we were mainly responsible for its birth.

Years later we tagged this war the "negative war," because it was, evident that it was only beneficial to the prison authorities, and it sunk us lower into the depths of depravity and foolishness. The circumstances surrounding this war were not unlikely, as unsavory wars among prisoners erupt identically in prisons across this country. Ironically, we became the miserable victims of each other to the sadistic delight of the very officials we claimed to despise.

The "negative war" was a full scale war several weeks after its beginning. It fed on its victim's own paranoia. It was an aberrant nightmare for me because I was the other half of its creation. Emotionally and mentally, I had to deal with this gnawing guilt; physically, I had to remain up to par in order to stay alive. In retrospect, I feel that my mental capacity was still within its embryonic stage. I was maturing but not in a speedy pace. I was swept with active force into a frenzied state of exaggerated pride in one's masculinity, but after repeatedly watching the blood and terror filled eyes of the victims, I was compelled to admit to myself that it all had become macabre and stupid.

Like most prison wars, this war started simple enough. The first two participants were me and another long term prisoner named, Malcolm "Mack" Jefferson. There were very few prisoners at Mecklenburg at this period. Mack, as Malcolm is known to his friends, was a medium sized, tan complexioned prisoner with a long history of violence against prisoners and guards. He had a pugnacious disposition and he was sensitive and emotional to the point of being irrational. Mack and James "Sporty" Washington allegedly shot and killed a prison guard during an escape attempt in 1971. This incident occurred at the Powhatan court house while they were waiting to be tried on minor charges which they had received at the Powhatan prison. The state claimed that Mack and Sporty overpowered the guard, took his service revolver and then shot him to death. Rumors from several guards, who were in the court room, hint that Mack and Sporty's guilt of this crime was questionable. Nevertheless, Mack was sentenced to die in the electric chair in December of

1972. Sporty received the same sentence two years later. Their notoriety expanded like a forest fire and their case promptly became a cause célèbre throughout Virginia.

I was confined to the Richmond State Penitentiary the year Mack was sentenced to die in the electric chair. There was pernicious unrest there, and the seat of my passions was at its pinnacle. The guards were physically abusing us daily, and the diminishing spirits of the, prisoners serving time there was displayed by the slow movements and slouching shoulders.

Mack became the spark that ignited the most fiery and significant riot this prison had ever produced. Two days after being sentenced to die, he had a violent confrontation with several guards on the compound while being escorted from a visit. He was shot in the face with a gas gun and sustained burns over a large part of his face. He was restricted to the prison hospital later that night, and this is where I first met him. During sick call I was able to talk with him and bring him items from the commissary. We became close comrades mainly because we were completely compatible in our hatred for prison guards. I easily committed myself to the campaign of his revenge.

In less than a week, spirits were renovated, minds were sharper, and hearts became stronger. Prisoners were rendezvousing all over the compound. Most prisoners there were recalcitrant, and a historical uprising was in the making.

Guards were first attacked in the kitchen and were downed with their own gas guns, then they were attacked arbitrarily and mercilessly throughout the compound. In an unrestrained fury we destroyed or attempted to destroy everything in front of us. The canteen and the back office which contained all of the classification papers were sacked. Fires were set everywhere; the levers that were used to control the cell doors were irreparably damaged, and weaker prisoners who were known informers were raped, beaten and stabbed. Hundreds of prisoners were united in the spirit of revenge and rebellion. Observing the relinquishment of these cruel prison guards was the closest I had ever come to experiencing a consciously spontaneous orgasm.

We overwhelmed the guards and within an hour this huge state prison was under siege. The assistant warden was held hostage inside the prison chapel by young convicts gripping baseball bats. We issued a long list of demands, emphasizing the ouster of specific guards who were known for their brutality. State troopers and Richmond police had surrounded the prison with shotguns. Richmond residents were filling the streets attempting to receive information concerning their loved ones inside. The older, more moderate prisoners were trying to negotiate with prison authorities, but we younger cats had become impulsive and incapable of compromise.

We dominated every facet of the prison for three days. During this period we strutted around wearing pieces of guard uniforms, concealed weapons in our belts, and staggered from one building to another in a drunken stupor from consuming rich portions of prison brew. Why the troopers and police did not storm the prison and kill us all still puzzles me today.

The third night, while most of us were drunk or exhausted, the state troopers, with military maneuvers, burst through our little amateur traps toting shotguns and recaptured the prison in less than 20 minutes. Later we were forced to run through a line of them while they taunted and kicked us. The principal characters of the riot were hauled to a dank basement and the prison was placed under total lock down.

Prison authorities agreed only to the demands that were of little or no importance. Most of the submissive prisoners were allowed to return to normal prison activities. The results of the riot: prisoners no longer were subjected to being locked up every day at five p.m., they were allowed personal TVs and radios, and the hated wall which had separated prisoners from their loved ones for over a hundred years was torn down. Several months later, the atmosphere was phantasmagoric, but eventually the conditions were surprisingly upgraded. The administrators even allowed select prisoners to have dances in the dining room with young women from the outside.

Mack was removed from the prison hospital and transferred back to the maximum security C Building. In 1972 there was no particular housing for death row prisoners in the Virginia prison system. I remained confined to the population in B basement for seven months before being released to the main population. After six months in main population, I was charged with first degree murder of another prisoner and sent to the detestable C Building population for the first time.

From 1973 until Mecklenburg opened in 1977, Mack and I remained close friends. We studied, observed, and demonstrated enthusiasm for the need to transform ourselves into mature revolutionaries. We refused to languish in self-pity or self-hatred, nor would we seek justice from a rank of people whom we felt were not capable of maintaining loyalty to it. We believed in no one but ourselves and the few who were striving with us, and we relentlessly worked to stimulate new thoughts in the collective mind of the C Building prisoners. No one, guard or prisoner, would have imagined in their wildest dreams that Mack and I were destined to become mortal enemies.

Prior to my transfer to Mecklenburg, Mack and I had made a vow to kill each other on sight. The origin of this conflict is too petty and insipid to dwell into, but at the time it was serious enough for me to permanently sever our comradeship.

Mack was transferred to Mecklenburg a month after my arrival. Rumors of our conflict, through the prison grape vine, was the latest topic and various prisoners who had claimed to be friends of both of us begin to choose sides. This news was like a gift from heaven for the Mecklenburg officials because it was right in step with their method of "divide and conquer."

Shortly after Building 1 and 2 were filled, the authorities moved the original six of us and a few others to different pods in both buildings. We were placed in the first phase of the three we were pressed to proceed through. In this phase we were confined to our cells steadily excluding an hour for outside recreation and five minutes for showers. We were allowed to call home only if there was evidence of sickness or death in the immediate family. Our only distractions from the monotonous misery were the personal radios we were allowed to possess.

Prison officials attempted to separate all of the convicts who were consistently disobedient but while moving us in such haste, they had mistakenly placed me in the same pod with Henry "Bobilly" Gorham, a reliable comrade whom I had become very close to in a short span of time. Bobilly was a giant of a man with enormous hands and the heart of a lion. More than half of the prisoners who'd served time with him feared his natural physical strength. He exuded power, confidence, and mental flexibility; these traits, coupled with his youth, quickness and volatile temperament, made him a formidable foe.

The "negative war" came to a head when sergeant Hudgen escorted two inmates who were in sympathy with Mack into our pod to clean up. Bobilly was upstairs in the shower behind a short curtain. We verbally warned him that two rats and a bald headed pig were in the pod. Bo sauntered from the shower with a large towel wrapped around his waist, then stood resolutely at the top of the stairs. He glared at them while the two inmates shakingly sold wolf tickets. A violent confrontation ensued: Bo was shot down by sergeant Hudgen with a stun gun, but he managed to astonishingly spring to his feet and stab Hudgen in his head. He stabbed one of the inmates in the face while the other rat scrambled through the gate which the control room guard had cracked for that purpose. Giving Bo verbal support, the rest of us were screaming to the top of our lungs. Sergeant Hudgen and the inmate who was stabbed in the face finally staggered out of the pod with echoes of our clapping hands behind them.

The negative war was established, and each group solemnly promised to destroy the other. From two convict's foolishness derived an ignominious war that witnessed 'too much blood, hatred and pain. Each group lost a sense of their limited principles and harbored no qualms about committing atrocities upon each other. During the period of 1977, 78, 79 and 80, there were attacks and counter attacks. We were winning, but the adrenaline rush which would impel me to jump and scream in my cell like a psychopath had long ago dissipated. I wanted it to end but it had become as uncontrollable and unsympathetic as a destructive, whirling wind.

This war aided prison officials in escalating their oppressive exercise of authority. While we were fighting each other, they were at the drawing board capitalizing on our mistakes. They were adroit at keeping each group at each other's throats. They would spread rumors telling members of each group outrageous lies to stir up their mutual animosities. Catron was .the main instigator. Every day during these disturbing years, he pranced around the Mecklenburg compound to sow tensions which would keep us divided and fighting among ourselves. Each white van that was driven out of the front gate, with a critically-wounded prisoner, would leave a sly smile etched on his face.

By 1979, members of each group were being set up by the guards. They were now well aware of which group each prisoner was loyal to. Mecklenburg's population had increased because the construction of Building 3, 4 and 5 was completed. There were at least three hundred prisoners, and more than half of them were involved in this war in one form or another. There were ample incidents where handcuffed prisoners were walked into a trap while being transferred from one pod or building to another. The guards were not concerned with a prisoner being hurt. They only watched the backs of each other. In truth, it would have been absurd for any prisoner to seek their protection, because even though they talked brave, whenever they saw the flash of a knife their balls shrunk like a deflated ballon

One hot day in June, 1979, the guards set it up for Mack and I to clash but they placed me in an unfavorable position. Prison officials were conducting a mass transfer, moving certain phases to different buildings. Phase I was being transferred to Building 5, and phase 3 was coming to Building 1. I was assigned to phase 1 and was forced to wear hand and ankle cuffs whenever I was escorted from one place to another. Mack was assigned to phase 3 and was allowed to work and walk around without any type restraints.

I was tensed as I emerged from my cell and noticed the two guards waiting to escort me acting suspiciously nervous. I precisely observed any movement close to me. I stepped from the recreation yard gate and instantly recognized the trap: out of the umpteen cement walkways and dirt paths stretched out in diversified directions of the compound, Mack and I were heading straight towards each other on the surface of the same walkway.

Bobilly was doing isolation time and could observe the scene from the rear window of his cell. "Watch out, Hashim ... they have you set up," he hollered from the window.

I stepped swiftly from the walkway to the lawn, bracing myself for an attack. The two guards with me remained stationary and never appeared surprised. Mack ran towards me like a wild beast. I watched only for his hands for a knife. He was so frantic in trying to strike me in the face that he missed repeatedly and only touched me with glancing blows. I was not able to maintain my balance while handcuffed from behind; but as soon as I hit the ground, two more convicts loyal to me lunged at Mack and began kicking at his groin. Seeing the situation getting out of hand without desired results, the guards rushed to us to restore order. Several phase 3 prisoners informed me later that Catron and Lt. Zimmerman were peering at this incident through a Building 3 window, punching each other with excitement.

A couple of weeks later, I encountered a small framed inmate on the recreation yard, at morning rec, who was deficient in vigor of mind and character. He was a suspected member of Mack's group, but we considered him as nothing but a cockroach. There was a trivial argument between us during a basketball game. It was over in seconds and I didn't give it a second thought. When the hour for recreation period was up, two guards entered the yard with sets of handcuffs. All five of us were handcuffed while this inmate, James Parker, was standing by the corner of the building with his hands free and a look of anger on his face. Still, the impact of the danger I was in did not fully register. I turned slightly to enter the building; seconds later I experienced a sharp pain at the left side of my chest. I twirled abruptly to see Parker standing there, clutching a short knife in trembling hands. Instinctively, I attacked him with my feet, kicking at him savagely. The knife was kicked out of his hands and the little hyena began retreating. The lack of courage of this inmate became evident, as I was getting the best of him while handcuffed from behind. Without warning, the two guards jumped me and slammed me roughly to the ground.

57

A reinforcement of guards darted into the yard and ordered the remaining prisoners to line up against the wall but these cats were all solid and contumacious to the max. They ignored the order and began attacking Parker with their feet. I was snatched to my feet, escorted to waiting van and rushed to the Memorial hospital in South Hill Virginia.

The next day, a control room guard in our pod managed to open four cell doors simultaneously during shower period. Bobilly and two comrades boldly slipped into Parker's cell. A desperate attack was waged inside that tiny cell. There were curses, hitting, wrestling and stomping, as Parker balled up in a fetal position to protect his face and groin.

I was not seriously injured; my stab wound only required nine stitches, but if my assailant had been blessed with balls I would have been killed. The guards never intervened until Parker was losing. They knew I had been stabbed, yet they never considered the possibility that my wound could have been potentially fatal. Attacking me while ignoring' my assailant was enough evidence for me of their intentions. This had also become customary reaction from the guards in each attack because most of them had marked the group in which they favored

Four months later Mack was demoted from phase 3 to phase 1 for receiving too many minor infractions. He was transferred to Building 5 in a pod quite some distance from me. A few weeks later there were transfers of many prisoners from one pod to another in Building 5. A convict named Thomas "Top Cat" Pen was placed in the same pod with Mack. This move sealed Mack's fate, and there's no doubt in my mind that a great number of prison officials were aware of this.

Top Cat was a five foot eleven, mild mannered, human fox, who was unanimously one of the most dangerous prisoners within the Virginia prison system. He was one of the craftiest prisoners I'd ever met. He was like a chameleon, as he could adopt any type behavior, no matter how ridiculous, to fit his surroundings or fake out his enemies. He had a superior IQ, and with all of his viciousness, he had a strong sense of control, which was baffling to some guards and prisoners alike. He would wait patiently for a victim like a hungry lion.

Thomas Pen had been a controversial figure in the Virginia prison system since his conviction in the late 1960s for six rapes and murders in Richmond, Virginia. He was sentenced to six life terms. During his long years of confinement, he had schemed his way out of numerous death traps, while setting them up for others. He was convicted in 1974 of brutally murdering another prisoner and sentenced to another life term in State Farm, Virginia. Only a very few prisoners or guards knew which group he was loyal to in this war because of his habitual secretiveness.

Mack was wickedly attacked! A comrade later informed me of what had happened. That evening, after the transfers were completed, prisoners in each pod were allowed showers. During this period, Mack stopped at Top Cat's cell in an attempt to feel him out. They rapped to each other for about fifteen minutes, and Top Cat convinced Mack that he was neutral regarding the war. Later that night they talked like close friends and exchanged magazines. The next morning, they strolled beside each other going to the recreation yard, whispering conspiratorially. They were un-handcuffed, then immediately begin walking up and down the course of the yard, exhibiting amicable gestures. Thirty minutes later, Mack went to the ping pong table and began playing, while Top Cat commenced walking the yard with another prisoner. Approximately twenty minutes prior to the termination of the recreation period, Top Cat moved rapidly behind Mack silently, with an emotionless face, and slashed his neck and face repeatedly with a gleaming, prison made razor. Mack screamed and turned with his hands in the air to shield his face. Top Cat slashed through Mack's faulty defense and continued to rip open his face and neck. Within seconds Mack seemed to be in a state of delirium. The prisoners close to the ping pang table dispersed out of honest fear of Top Cat and his unpredictability. Blood was spattering all over the ping pong table as it spurted from Mack's wounds. Moments later, Top-Cat was subdued by the Pert Team, and Mack was escorted quickly to a prison van to be rushed to the South Hill Memorial hospital. Bobilly and a few more comrades saw Mack leaping into the back of the van with a white bloodied towel wrapped around his head, and they gave Top Cat a standing ovation.

Mack was a fairly handsome man. The burns he had received to his face prior to the State Pen riot had healed sufficiently. The lower half of his face was harshly disfigured from the sequence of Top Cat's, attack. He no longer looked the same, and this inevitably affected his character. His movements were slower when he talked he was barely audible, he was no longer extroverted, and his domineering temperament had dissolved.

The war roared on without interval. The appalling Parade of violence confined within the towering gun towers and barbed wire fences of Mecklenburg never touched a nerve on the outside. The governor and prison director's lack of initiative stimulated the prison official's burning desire to keep the war alive. Prisoners were being mutilated by each other in a war which was now expanding to other Virginia, institutions, yet there was never even a hint of a fair inquiry by the impassive politicians or the numbskull prison authorities

We were like a multitude of frenzied killer sharks, devouring each other, while the shark hunters were capturing, killing, and trying to control every aspect of our lives. Our attention span relating to the brutality of the guards had become very brief. Our actions had become synonymous with the actions of distinctive blacks living in the teeming ghettos of America. Their aggression is misdirected. They kill and maim each other from the emotion of self-hatred and a deep seated fear of the true architect of their misery. They deem the oppressor a being too powerful and isolated to reach, thus they seek a weaker and closer target. Most of them harbor faint hearts and refuse to act directly against the oppressor. As a result, intra group violence and disunity is accepted as being normal by them.

We maintained that we were vividly aware of ourselves and our trying situation, but like most prisoners who engage in the despicable act of destroying each other, rather than confronting the source of their oppression, we were losing needed and special traits in the process. We were not stable or together enough at the time to realize how dull in the mind we appeared to our tormentors. Prison authorities used this war to free from guilt or blame the creation of Mecklenburg, and this war gave them and the Virginia public the incentive to keep Mecklenburg functioning with the depressive doctrine of "behavior modification."

Death Row Escape

*"This is a completely cruel and perverse state of affairs,
more keeping with the frenzied ignorance of the middle
ages than the allegedly enlightened and humane spirit of a
late 20th century democracy."*

Bob Herbert

In 1980, two blood brothers, James and Linwood
Briley, were being tried for several murders in Richmond,
Virginia. They were two individuals among thousands who
had attempted to adapt to the concrete jungles of the
ghetto. Their trials and alleged heinous crimes were
occasionally described in the Richmond daily newspapers.
There seemed to be nothing extra-ordinary about either
one. Yet within four years they would be admired, loathed,
and talked about more than any other two prisoners in
Virginia history. They would put the Mecklenburg
institution on the map, and promote the most disastrous

era for the Virginia politicians and prison administrators. They were fated to become two prominent nemeses of the Virginia prison system.

I recalled seeing photos of these two brothers in the Richmond Times Dispatch. They were always well groomed and immaculately dressed in expensive looking suits. JB, as James was addressed by friends and associates possessed an innocent boyish smile, while Linwood was stone faced with a penetrating stare. From my rudimentary inspection of these photos, JB seemed care free and flamboyant, as Linwood appeared introverted and secretive. I would discover years later that this inspection was basically accurate. Their outstanding bond derived more from the concept of the thickness of blood than the equivalence of ideas or character.

The black communities in Richmond were crumbling from the effects of black on black crime, and the people existing in these communities had become disgusted with the feelings of sympathy towards black predators for the sole reason that they were black. But James and. Linwood's convictions and subsequent death sentences motivated a surge of mixed emotions within these communities because there was an uncertainty of opinion in reference to their guilt. The focal point of this doubt was the people's paranoia of the racist Richmond police. These police officers depreciated themselves among the people by their actions and attitudes towards them. Many Richmond blacks felt that James and Linwood were set up because the police claimed that they had been tailing them for weeks and were on their tail the night they allegedly entered a North Side house and murdered a child, pregnant woman and man who lived there. They also claimed that they were parked outside the house during the incident, and that they observed James, Linwood, their younger brother, Anthony, and future informant, Duncan Meekins, leaving the house and entering a car with stolen goods in their arms. Convictions were obtained from the confession of Meekins and the testimonies of the police.

JB and Linwood were sentenced to die in the electric chair for murder and rape. JB was sentenced to die twice for killing Judith Diane Barton and her son,

Harvey. Anthony was given a life sentence because of his youth. Sixteen year old Meekins received a life sentence because of his confession and cooperation in testifying against the three brothers for the prosecution.

Neighbors, relatives and friends openly refused to believe that these three easy going brothers were involved in such repulsive crimes. Four weeks after the sentences were handed down; Meekins name was twin to human feces throughout most of the black neighborhoods.

The crimes in which the Briley brothers were linked to, based on the newspaper accounts of Meekins' confession, would cause any normal person to yield to revulsion. Following is a list of the criminal events in chronological order:

March 21, 1979: Anthony and Linwood robbed a vending company serviceman. After robbing him, they abducted him in his car. Later they shot him to death and left his body in the car.

March 31, 1979: Linwood and Meekins were fuming over a dispute with Edric Clark over drugs. They went to his house and Linwood shot him to death with a rifle.

April 9, 1979: Linwood and Anthony follow an old woman who'd just left her apartment in the West End section. Meekins and Linwood grab her in front of the apartment and rob her. Linwood rapes her, and then shoots her dead with a gun.

July 3, 1979: Linwood, Meekins and Anthony observe a seventeen year old male tampering with Linwood's car. The youth is beaten by them. Linwood kills him by hitting him in the head with a cinder block.

Sept. 14, 1979: The group now including JB, assault disc jockey "Johnny G Gallaher." Gallaher was robbed and then driven to Mayo's Island, where Linwood killed him by shooting him in the back with a rifle.

Sept. 30, 1979: The group accosted an aged nurse in front of her apartment in western Henrico. JB grabs her pocketbook after killing her with a blow to the •head with a baseball bat.

Oct. 6, 1979: Blanche I. Page and her boarder were piped to death by Linwood in the Page home. Garner's back was later set on fire by the group.

Oct. 14, 1979: Linwood, JB and Meekins entered the East End apartment of Thomas Saunders. Meekins shoots Saunders dead as a favor for a friend.

Their last alleged acts of brutality occurred on the night of Oct. 19, 1979, and it sent shock waves throughout the black communities.

2301 Barton Ave. was the home of Harvey Wilkerson and his common law wife, Judy Barton; He grew up in the same North Side neighborhood with the Briley brothers. Wilkerson and Ms. Barton were both employed at Interbake Foods in Richmond. Their relationship had survived close to seven years, and they were negotiating to buy a house in South Richmond. Their son, Harvey, was five years old, and Ms. Barton was expecting their second child in April.

Prior to the date of these murders, JB had been out of prison on parole for two months. According to the police, on the night of the final murders they had the gang under surveillance. They said that they had sat unknowingly in a squad car and waited while these people were being savagely murdered.

According to Meekins, the group knew Wilkerson well and was doing drug related business with him. Wilkerson admitted them in his house without any sign of suspicion. The group later fed mice to Wilkerson's pet boa constrictors and participated in light chatter. Then they made their move. Pulling a gun on Wilkerson, the three brothers tied him up with electrical tape after taking a gun from him. While part of the group ransacked the house, placing stereo equipment at the top of the stairs, other members of the group dragged a bound and gagged Ms. Barton into the kitchen, where they repeatedly raped her on the floor.

While JB was in the kitchen, Meekins watched Wilkerson and allowed him to speak to his son. JB sauntered back into the living room from the kitchen and told Meekins to put the child on the sofa. A member of the group then slipped a choke chain (similar to the type used to restrain dogs) around the child's neck and covered the adult victims with sheets.

Linwood, left to start the car. JB later shot Ms. Barton in the head. He handed the gun to Meekins, who didn't hesitate in shooting Wilkerson dead before running out of the door. Then they drove away and soon realized that they were being followed through the techniques of a stolen police scanner. They eluded the police officers.

The bodies of Wilkerson, Ms. Barton and their son were discovered at their home on Oct. 21. The autopsy of Wilkerson revealed that three butcher knives, a pair of scissors and a meat fork had been stabbed into his back.

On Oct. 22, the police stated in a Times Dispatch article that they held an emergency meeting and decided to take a warrant out on Linwood. He was under suspicion for other crimes, and police officers watching him the night of the murders said that they had heard shots. A few hours after the warrant was issued, Linwood, his father and Meekins were found in a car by detectives. Linwood's father was released, and Meekins was held for questioning.

Meekins was interrogated extensively, but he refused to talk until his father and mother arrived at police headquarters. The intimidated youth confessed, and police promptly apprehended JB and Anthony.

Meekins was sent to a Federal witness protection program after the convictions. Anthony was received at the State Penitentiary population in Richmond, and JB and Linwood arrived at the recently opened death row section at Mecklenburg, located in Building-1, pod c. Almost every prisoner, prison official, and Richmond resident would get caught up in the aura of these two brother's lives from the aftermath of one of the most daring and clever escapes from the tight security of death row.

Before JB and Linwood arrived at Mecklenburg I was discharged to the streets. I had served a lengthy sentence for armed robbery. Emotionally, I was a human wreck, but I summoned all of my inner strength in an attempt to conceal it.

The transition from Mecklenburg to the streets was not smooth. I was now thirty two years old. My daughter, Kim, (the love of my life) was fourteen. I had no job prospect, no money, and no place to stay except my father's house. My only emotional satisfaction stemmed from the stimulating relationship I shared with my daughter, and the dim light of the future seemed to fade with each passing hour of this so called freedom.

This is the situation with ninety percent of the prisoners being released from prisons today. Most crimes are committed for economic reasons, and because newly released prisoners usually are strapped for money and poorly qualified for decent jobs, they often return to crime to support themselves or their families.

I was no exception, but from the perception of my revolutionary consciousness, I could no longer attach myself to any form of regular street crime which would bring harm to innocent people. Thus I began to rob drug dealers, people whom I held in contempt. Terrorizing these cowardly leeches somewhat rejuvenated me and made me feel like a soldier again.

I was arrested several times but was always released because the drug dealers would never press robbery charges against me. The Norfolk police despised me because many of them were working with the dealers, as most Norfolk dealers are undercover informers. I knew I was fated to either be killed or to add to the high rate of recidivism, but I was not willing to stop. My rampage ended with my arrest for robbery and wounding of a sailor who was dealing drugs. Exhaustively fed up with me, Norfolk detectives promised prostitute immunity for her crimes if she testified against me; they rigged up a weak but strong enough case against me to get me sentenced to fifty one years in prison. I had been in the streets less than a year!

Back in prison, the Classification Committee at the State Pen recommended my placement in the dreadful C-Building. They reasoned that there were participants of the "negative war" now mingled in each Virginia institution, and that they could not take the hazardous chance of placing me in any population. I lingered in C-Building in limbo for a year, then was transferred to Mecklenburg. Catron was now assistant warden and he didn't want to deal with me again. A week later the Mecklenburg Classification Committee transferred me to the State Farm in State Farm, Virginia.

I felt like a patient suffering from post-traumatic stress syndrome. I was jumpy and uncomfortable around more than one person. I remained to myself and brooded everyday over the manner I had failed my duties as a revolutionary and a father. Two months later .I was in a van on my way back to Mecklenburg for attacking a prison nurse with an iron pipe.

I was instantly housed in the segregation section of Building-1 in Mecklenburg. This section was just a short distance from the death row pod which held nine prisoners. A week later I met JB as I was being escorted by two guards to the recreation yard. We were walking by the death row pod when suddenly this tall, smooth faced guy ran to the bars.

"Hashim Khan... what's up, man? I heard you were back up here. Come to the back window when you get outside cause I want to rap to you."

I stared at him wondering where he knew me from. I also did not immediately recognize him because his hair was much longer than it had been in the newspaper photos.

"Yeah, I showed a week ago," I responded. "I'll hollor at you when I get outside." A few death row prisoners whom I knew spoke to me and I gave them the power raised fist as I continued to walk towards the recreation yard door.

While I was on the recreation yard, JB and an old friend of mine, Willie "T" Turner, who was scheduled to die for killing a jewelry store owner during a robbery, came to the back window. JB explained to me that he and Bobilly had become close, and that Bo had assured him that I was good people. He said that he also liked everything he had heard about me. Then T, as Turner is' called by most people, began rapping to me about his case and before I knew it my hour was up.

Later that night a guard, assigned to the death row pod, slipped a brown legal envelop under my cell door. I opened it and found a letter from JB and two sticks of marijuana. The letter was brief but to the point. He conveyed to me that he had made substantial progress in utilizing the corruptness of the Mecklenburg guards. He had many of these guards on his payroll and this enabled him to obtain handcuff keys, vital information, drugs, and any other' necessity profitable to him and the brothers. I was sort of skeptical about the validity of this information, but in the coming months I would learn that this first letter was an understatement.

JB was affable, soft spoken, and extremely shrewd. This combined with his daily display of effervescence made him a captivator with unnatural effectiveness. Some of the most unreasonable and vicious Mecklenburg guards liked him and spoke highly of him. I had never witnessed anything of this magnitude at Mecklenburg before. Here was a condemned convict who was allegedly linked to twelve murders, and prison guards were patting him on the back, playing cards with him, purchasing contraband for him, and even divulging secrets about the security procedures of the institution.

Linwood remained aloof and unapproachable. We only spoke a very few words to each other. He seemed more involved than JB in fighting his death sentence through appeals. JB and I gradually became close friends. We exchanged letters every night, and he would purchase, sweets from the canteen which I would buy from him with cigarettes. (Segregated prisoners were allowed to purchase only cosmetics and cigarettes from the canteen).

When JB opened up in his thoughts and ideas, the depth of his intelligence enthralled me. He never was subtle about his feelings towards dying in the electric chair, and he continually reiterated a candid assessment of his predicament. He never believed in the judicial system of America; escape to him was the only logical method for a prisoner to perfect and pursue. He was absorbed in the challenge of escaping from the supposedly escape proof institution that so many administrators and politicians were bragging about.

JB and Linwood had a vast number of female admirers. Linwood definitely was no slouch in this department; he was a charming ladies' man in his own quiet way. They daily received an ample amount of mail from young women intimate, perfumed letters with lascivious suggestions. Earlier an attractive woman was charged with aiding and abetting in an attempt escape by concealing a loaded gun in the bathroom of the visiting room for them. She was one of their many luscious visitors.

In the autumn of 1983 I was finally promoted to phase 11 and transferred to Building-5. The political consciousness of Mecklenburg prisoners was now predominating. The "negative war was reaching its termination; I could gratefully feel it. More convicts were agreeing that it should be discarded because it exposed persistent folly in our response to tyranny. With this intoxicating revelation influencing my attitude, I was not able to survive under the needling pressure of behavior modification. Two and a half months later, I was transferred back to Building-1 for assaulting a guard with my fist.

In January of 1984, JB's letters reflected his desperation and persevering loyalty towards Linwood. Linwood was scheduled to die in the electric chair on the night of October 12, 1984. JB rambled unceasingly about escape, the unfairness of capital punishment regarding blacks and he expressed the fact that it was inconsequential to the governor or any Virginia politician whether he or Linwood were guilty or not, because all they wanted was more blood, as the capitalist could not remain powerful without our blood dripping from his fangs. He was still poised and refined, but I believe his intensity during this period was the impetus for them to speed up the almost impeccable plans that would materialize on the night of May 31.

Every day the prisoners on death row who were involved in the escape plans were having group meetings, taking each other's ideas into account, even though JB and Linwood were the accepted master minds. These meetings led to uneasiness on the row, and notes from uninvolved death row inmates began to reach the authorities. Twice in April prison officials were warned that several condemned men would attempt an escape. The warden ordered a complete "lock down" on the row. For five days the pod was searched for weapons, and none of the prisoners were allowed to leave their cells. No weapons were found.

A second note was received a few weeks later and the warden brought in Virginia State Police surveillance experts to conduct another search for weapons. Again, nothing was found. Prison administrators would not discover until months after the condemned men had escaped that tiny holes were professionally drilled in the walls of the death row cells to adequately conceal weapons. The walls had been painted over several times.

At about nine o'clock on the night of May 31, there was an aggravating noise level in the segregation pod. The guards had not made their routine rounds within the last two hours and this was very unusual. The prisoners were hollering for soap, toilet paper, writing paper, and essentials only the guards are allowed to pass out in segregation. I noticed that there wasn't even a guard stationed in the control room of the pod. I knew something strange was happening, but I didn't connect it to JB or death row because JB was always vague about the exact date of the escape. He also never disclosed any definite details in relation to its execution. My inquisitiveness had me pacing the floor of my cluttered cell like a caged, restless tiger; so many questions hovered in my mind.

Approximately an hour later, in the midst of raucous screaming, T and another death row prisoner appeared in front of the bars of our pod. They were clutching guard clubs and wearing riot helmets. It was happening! It was really happening! I stood immobile at my cell door for a few seconds, as an animated sensation caressed every nerve of my body a unique sensation which I've never felt before or since. The pod became so quiet that the humming of the air conditioner sounded like the engine of a 727 jet.

T quickly explained to us that they (death row) were in the process of escaping, and that they needed at least another half an hour of quietness and cooperation from us. He divulged the situation of the guards and nurses who were now hostages secured at the lower section of the death row pod then he stated confidently that some of them would be gone before eleven o' clock. He also revealed the possibility that some of us would be released from our cells. This suggestion was later vetoed because most of them felt that we would cause a heat drawing disruption and hinder the success of the escape. We gave them our verbal approval, and then they walked back towards the action, flashing victory signs for us.

The things we were raising hell to attain prior to T's arrival were now so insignificant that we easily dismissed them and just waited in stunned silence for the culmination of the escape that would knock the Mecklenburg prison to its knees!

Thirty five minutes later, whispering to comrade "Tee" Jackson on the vent about the impending escape, I was interrupted by the shouting of a convict called "Shorty World," who resided on the bottom tier. He was telling everyone to hurry to the back window of their cells. I rushed to the window, and during my lifetime don't think it will ever be possible to fathom the feelings stirred within me from what I witnessed at that moment: JB, Linwood and four other condemned men, dressed in guard uniforms and riot gear, were leisurely walking across the yard carrying a stretcher. I didn't know it at the time but later reports confirmed that this was all a part of an elaborate ruse. The female guard in the guard tower was deceived into believing that they were Mecklenburg guards bringing a bomb out of the death row pod. The fake bomb was a television set from the death row day room, covered by a blanket.

Phase 111 prisoners in Building-5 began shouting obscenities at them from the windows, calling them "stinking pigs" and "faggot motherfuckers." One of the condemned men laughed, another one occasionally sprayed the fake bomb with a fire extinguisher. As they walked closer to their freedom, I recognized JB's bouncy walk and I knew Linwood had to be somewhere close to him. When they reached the sally port, their last serious obstacle; the tension had my body rigid and soaked with sweat.

They casually carried the television set to an awaiting van at the sally port, and then instructed the guard to stand clear of the bomb and he complied. They silently walked the last few yards to the van, threw the stretcher through the open rear door and jumped in. The six of them drove out of the gate, just as smooth as silk and as sweet as cotton candy.

Mecklenburg prison had been presented to the public, especially the residents of Boydton, a town nearby, as an intricate prison structure that would never be stung by the humiliation of even one escape. Until May 31, 1984, this presentation appeared to be sound. Thus the varied explanations to the public regarding the escape, which contained traces of stupidity and naiveté, were expected by us. Prison director Robert M. Landon, said that repeated mistakes by prison officials, errors he termed— "a breakdown in human engineering", and enabled the six convicted murderers to escape Virginia's death row at Mecklenburg. Landon declined to speculate on whether prison officials would be disciplined for the lapses, but insisted that procedures at the facility should have prevented the breakout.

This made me laugh because I knew that without guard corruption, without fundamental inside aid, even the knowledge JB and Linwood had would not have been sufficient to accomplish successfully an escape of this caliber. The escape became a hypothesis of intrigue for the unfortunate people who had to listen to Landon's feverish attempts to distort the truth. A few days after the escape so called experts began probes involving the constellation of issues connected to it, but strangely the issues of guard corruption was never mentioned until a condemned inmate, Dennis W. Stockton, revealed portions of it in a diary he had sent to the Virginia Pilot newspaper of Norfolk.

An inside version of the escape was later given to me by a condemned comrade who had decided not to leave with the six fugitives. From his recollection, he wove an interesting account of the once anonymous two brothers who had become infamous overnight: On May 30, JB conferred with the other participants and emphatically announced his urgency to leave because of the drawing dead line of Linwood's execution date. Everyone agreed with him but there were minor conflicts concerning the initial stage of the escape. Determined to follow through after such a long period of planning, they all stifled their complaints and prepared themselves mentally for the next night. JB and Linwood had hundred dollar bills in their pockets, and they had pinpointed their destination after the success of the escape; the other four were ambiguous about this.

Their first and most essential reward for their endeavor was the guard's error of failing to count or counting incorrectly the condemned men after the yard recreation period was over. A prisoner was missing; if this had been swiftly detected the escape may have never succeeded.

Earl Clanton Jr. had ducked into a rest room for prison employees while the prisoners were coming in from the recreation yard. He locked the door and just sat and waited. The guards tried to open the rest room door twice within the next 40 minutes; even though it remained locked with no one answering inside, they still insouciantly responded to the situation.

About 8:40 the control room guard brought a book to JB, leaving the control room door open. Clanton then ran out of the rest room and into the control room, where he worked the electrical switches to free the prisoners from the day room. The prisoners possessed deadly looking weapons and they overpowered the four guards in the pod and tied them up after stripping them to their underclothes.

In the next hour, eight guards and two nurses arrived at the death row area and were captured. A few of them were called by the prisoners imitating guards; others arrived on their own. JB and another prisoner argued vehemently because one of the nurses was being raped in the cell. They also argued about killing or allowing the hostages to live. There would later be a twisted confession from a condemned, non-involved rat, making himself a hero to gain immunity.

At 10:30, the prisoners paged a guard outside the building and he phoned the pod. Derick Peterson put a towel over the receiver to disguise his voice, then told him to bring the van to the prison gate so a bomb found in the pod could be removed. A knife was held at the throat of a lieutenant as they forced him to call the tower guard and order her to open the double gate sally port, leaving the prison exit wide open.

15 Minutes later, the six desperate. Prisoners, JB and Linwood in front, walked out of Building-1 as another prisoner held the door open from the main control room. The success of this escape would kindle one of the most massive and jumbled man hunts in the history of this country.

Manhunt

The next day, June 1, Virginia newspapers did not placate the embarrassment of Mecklenburg authorities. Anger was voiced by all of the major news reporters. Everyone seemed bewildered with the smoothness of the escape. Many Boydton residents stated that they felt like victims of con-artists because they were duped into believing that an escape of this nature was impossible at Mecklenburg. Catron, Lt. Zimmerman and Gary Bass, the third warden since the opening of Mecklenburg, were rashly attempting to extricate themselves from direct blame. Mecklenburg's previous protected secrets were being exposed, and we were more than pleased with the oppressor's discomfort.

According to news reports, the six fugitives drove across the North Carolina line to the town of Warrenton, where they ditched the prison van behind a school. Shortly after midnight two of them tried to commandeer a car and the police were alerted. Peterson and Clanton had separated from the rest. Lost in Warrenton, a very small town, they had no car, a small amount of money and no contacts. The search was now so heavy that they had no alternative but to disappear from the streets. They ducked into a coin laundry and hastily purchased soda and cheese and were arrested in the laundry without resistance about an hour later.

There was a massive search conducted in the area, but JB, Linwood, Tuggle and Jones were long gone in a stolen pickup truck. They headed north, passing through Richmond on an interstate. JB and Linwood eventually separated from Tuggle and Jones; Philadelphia was their goal. Tuggle and Jones kept going north. Their goal was the Canadian border.

What aided all four of them was the numerous "sightings" in Canada and other places. Search teams were searching for them in cities and towns hundreds of miles from where they actually were. Panic and impatience were making the search teams act like Keystone cops. Police in Virginia and North Carolina tracked down a great number of leads on June 2, which proved to be futile. Several hundred lawmen were now joined in the search. Portsmouth police, assisted by the FBI, exchanged gunshots with a suspect who they claimed looked like JB. JB was nowhere near Portsmouth, Virginia.

None of the tips from people who believe they had spotted the escapees panned out, and this aroused the anxiety of law enforcement officials.

A Virginia Beach dispatcher stated: "Everybody sees them, but none of them have turned up yet?

Governor Charles S. Rob made public that he was authorizing a $10,000 reward for information leading to the apprehension of the fugitives.

Virginia and North Carolina residents were given a toll free number to call in case they had any information.

On the morning of June 2, a cab driver reported to authorities that he was forced to drive 100 miles from Durham to Salisbury North Carolina, by an armed man who fit the description of Lem Tuggle. The cab was found later about 50 miles north of Charlotte North Carolina. Several officers with bloodhounds later searched every building and every abandoned car or house in that area.

A spokesman for the North Carolina Department of Crimes Control and Public Safety stated that at this period searches were confined to three are: A wooded section south of Warrenton. An area south of Warrenton where a dog found a .Virginia Corrections

Department jacket believed to have been abandoned by one of the fugitives. An area near Kearney North Carolina, in Franklin County, where there was a report of a sighting of one of the escapees.

An FBI spokesman tried to clear the existing rumors coming from Portsmouth by announcing that it would be absolutely impossible for either of the Brileys to be in Portsmouth an hour after the sighting near Warrenton. He said they were discounting the notion that James or Linwood was in Portsmouth.

The Briley brother's names were now household words. Neighbors in every city were discussing them, and keeping outdoor lights on while checking window bolts and door locks.

"Everybody is talking about it," said one neighbor of Portsmouth. "1 don't think the people around here will be satisfied until they are caught."

Two Mecklenburg employees who had been threatened by the escapees expressed relief that they survived the ordeal. One of them who spent several hours as a hostage said that he was "scared to death" because he knew he was under the complete control of dangerous men who had nothing to lose. Both employees declined to be identified or elaborate on details of the escape. They did both agree that the Breakout shook assumptions that the maximum security prison was escape proof.

"This escape shows there is either something wrong with the personnel or the construction of the building", said a member of the State Crime Commission. "How could persons plan something like that and then execute it so perfectly? It must have taken a lot of planning."

State prison authorities were still rallying in their defense. "We've got a pretty good escape record, we really do, notwithstanding the terrible events of Thursday night," said a corrections spokesman.

On June 3 the newspapers gave explicit details of the fugitive's crimes, which increased the public's mounting fear.

Tuggle and Jones had stopped in Vermont, found a tent and camped out. After spending several nights near the border, they separated. Tuggle headed south. On June 8, Jones, while talking on the phone was persuaded by his mother to turn himself in.

The same day Tuggle robbed a gift shop with a knife to attain money for gasoline. Approximately 45 minutes later, a local cop blocked the path of the stolen pickup truck and Tuggle was captured without further struggle.

Search teams were still trying to locate the whereabouts of JB and Linwood. The search had spread up the east coast. Quebec had also joined the regular team in Canada.

The convicts at Mecklenburg called Lem Davis Tuggle "Big Tug," as he was medium height, weighing 230 pounds. At Mecklenburg I knew him as a generous, mild mannered, humorous fellow. He was the only white prisoner involved in the escape. After his capture, he was placed in the basement of the State Pen with Jones. The chamber that houses the state's electric chair was close by. On July 10, Tuggle was granted the first interview by any of the captured escapees. He proposed no needful insight into the preparations preceding the escape but his recital was interesting.

He'd planned to be in the Canadian wilderness by now, hiding out in a cabin, trapping wildlife and just keeping to himself. He was going to stay there the next 20 or 30 years.

"My only mistake when I got out of that prison was having to rob that lady in Vermont. If I'da had 50 more miles, I wouldn't be sitting here right now." There was a trace of depression in his voice.

He criticized conditions in Virginia prisons, described his stint of freedom as a "dream come true," and portrayed himself and his cohorts as "desperate men."

"I can't speak for anyone but myself and about anyone else but myself. The main thing I want to get across is that there was no violence during the escape. We had ample opportunity to have plenty of violence and there wasn't any. I made an agreement not to hurt anyone before or after the escape. I wanted to prove 'em all wrong. The escape was the only way. The appeal court is run by what's in the record, and if you don't do something to prove yourself, you can forget about it."

After the van wheeled away from Mecklenburg, Tug recalled a strange mixture of clapping and praying among the six condemned men as they sped toward North Carolina. 'We were extremely happy," he said.

Tug also refused to discuss why four of them doubled back toward Virginia and on toward Philadelphia and Vermont in a stolen pickup truck. They had passed within a few miles of Mecklenburg.

Tug's closing statements were: "They claim we're killers that would kill anybody and we're not that type of people.

We're just plain, ordinary people... we're just victims of society."

Two weeks after the escape, there were Briley tee shirts, Briley songs, and many Virginians indicating their desire for them to never be captured,. The bank robber, John Dillinger, had stated that he would rather be famous for a year and die than live for a life time in anonymity. Dillinger received his year, but JB and Linwood, through one daring act, had almost surpassed this gangster in notoriety.

The Briley brothers had made it to Philadelphia, where they settled in a black neighborhood. Their activities were normal; they made friends without any outward signs of nervousness. They did odd jobs during the day and were given a place to sleep in a garage. Residents of the neighborhood accepted them as two courteous Georgians, Lucky and Slim, down on their luck. On June 19, JB, Linwood and an uncle of theirs, were among a crowd of people at a barbecue outing in front of a car repair shop. The FBI disrupted the outing with shotguns and ordered everyone to lie face down on the ground. JB and Linwood were handcuffed, hustled to a squad car and driven to a Philadelphia jail.

Rumors immediately hit the prison grapevine concerning the grounds for their capture. Tuggle was accused of "snitching," so were girlfriends and others. The FBI's official report claimed that they had been watching the Briley's uncle, Johnnie Lee Council, who was a resident of Philadelphia, and that they had racked a call made from Philadelphia to an acquaintance of the Brileys in New York. In all probability, the truth will stay buried in the FBI files.

On June 22, total elation swept through the Mecklenburg population from the news that Catron, who had been promoted to assistant warden, Warden Bass and Lt. Zimmerman, were all being disciplined and transferred from Mecklenburg. The department had accused Catron of withholding information about the escape, and failing to supervise properly the guards who might have foiled the escape. The embarrassing breakout had eliminated the two chief tyrants whom we had been battling persistently for eight years.

In September the composure of Mecklenburg officials was further disrupted by a diary that was written by death row inmate, Dennis W. Stockton. Stockton, an odd looking prisoner, sent the diary to the Virginia Pilot newspaper and requested its publication. It was later published in full text;

it triggered such an uproar that Stockton had to be moved to death row isolation for his own protection. The diary covered more than a year on Mecklenburg's death row and gave a detailed account of plans for the mass escape. He hurt the already tarnished image of the Mecklenburg regime by accusing several guards of smuggling in contraband to prisoners. He made incriminating statements about prisoners and Mecklenburg employees, and told of drug and alcohol abuse, homosexuality and treachery among death row prisoners.

Stockton said that he realized that he was putting his life in danger by allowing his diary to be published, but he said that there was a cover up about the escape and he wanted the story told. The only guard actually named in the printed accounts pleaded guilty to smuggling marijuana into the prison and was sentenced to 12 months in jail.

The diary was adamantly criticized by prison officials and governor Robb. The new acting warden, 'Sherman Townley, said' that Stockton only jeopardized himself, and that he had not read anything in the published accounts of the diary that would warrant another investigation at Mecklenburg. Governor Robb challenged the accuracy of the diary. He said the diary was "revealing" but at least partly inaccurate. His statement was based on polygraph tests given to Stockton that didn't check out at critical points. When a reporter asked Robb where he believed the diary erred, Robb directed him to the head of the investigative unit of the state police.

Jay Cochran, the head of the unit, said the discrepancies dealt with "specific issues concerning guards" involvement in delivery of weapons or drugs" to prisoners. When Stockton was asked about the role of various guards during the polygraph test, Cochran said, "Specific responses were untruthful."

A ranking member of the Senate Appropriations Committee's corrections subcommittee said he believed the diary revelations would affect how the legislature acts on corrections next year. "These articles will probably cause some discussion," he said. "When you're talking to citizens, they find what they read shocking and unbelievable. But when you're talking to legislators and staff people who have dealt with the system before, to them it's not so surprising."

The accuracy of the complete diary was not the issue. I found many inaccurate statements in the diary, and this inmate came across like a lonely man seeking attention but

I believe governor Robb's motive for attacking the diary involved his willingness to keep the public from dwelling into the corruptness and intellect bankruptcy of Mecklenburg authorities.

We were singing and conversing exuberantly in celebration of the fall of Catron and Zimmerman, but if we could have foreseen future events, the duration of this bliss would have been short lived.

Chastisement: Mecklenburg Style

"One condition that hasn't changed in prisons over the years has been the brutality."

Bonnie Kerness

Late one scorching evening in the summer of 1978, I was gazing through the recreation yard fence at a heart breaking but common activity at Mecklenburg. A prisoner was being dragged down the walkway of Building 5. Seven guards were attacking him with Billy clubs and gas guns. While he cried out piteously in agony, they passionately battered his head, face and body. This prisoner was hand and ankle cuffed during this grisly attack. As usual, Catron was presiding over this incident with his arms folded, staring at the beating with his twisted, and hideous smile.

The Supreme Court had abolished "corporeal punishment" in prisons, but the Mecklenburg regime was practicing it with impunity. Too many Mecklenburg prisoners were losing their heart and fire after a compilation of life threatening attacks by prison guards. I could see the resignation in their eyes. Unity among us ceased to exist, and we had eased into a strange state of madness which produced our situation to that of laboratory animals that begin to annihilate one another when conditions become unbearable. Torture and corporeal punishment turns prisoners into psychopathic individuals; engaging in violence becomes a temptation to them almost like a narcotic.

There were still isolated attacks against the guards by prisoners, and Catron was determined to eradicate it by keeping us trapped within this cloud of ignorance and frightening us into submissiveness. A series of abominable acts that would make Charles Manson shutter, were obtrusively unleashed on us. The horrible things that were done to us burned itself disgracefully into Virginia prison legend. Beatings became regular occurrences, coupled with tear gassings, denial of food, and forceful injections of Thorazine and other tranquilizing drugs. The most shocking was their policy of chaining us to the beds of our cells for days.

Paul Coomer, a white convict with a history of being non-cooperative, was punished in this obnoxious fashion for three full days. The bed mattress was placed on the floor for his usage. He was hand and ankle cuffed during this entire period. Chains linked to these cuffs were secured through the holes of the steel bed bunk. The length of the chain enabled him to move only inches from his bed. He was not allowed to bathe, brush his teeth or use the toilet. His clothing was never changed and his cell was never cleaned. He urinated and defecated in his pants, and was required to lie in it while the odor saturated his skin. The nauseating heat and stench draw irritating flies that frequently swarmed him. He was fed infrequently, and when he was fed his food tray was intentionally kicked towards him, spilling most of its contents. To consume his food he had to lap and nibble at it like a dog!

Some prisoners went berserk under this manner of torture. Twenty four hours a day we were bombarded with their recurring screams. These screams were also excruciating mental pain for the rest of us. There was nothing we could do to divert the attention of our wretchedness.

One of the key perpetrators of guard brutality at Mecklenburg was a short, stocky, bald headed black guard named Powell. He was a sergeant who would have eagerly licked Catron's anus if he had been ordered to do so. He was also a former member of the cold blooded guard force of C Building. This major flunky shuffled behind Catron and Lt. Zimmerman from pod to pod, building to building, with an imbecilic, Uncle Tom grin on his face.

Sergeant Powell's sadistic behavior was general among black prison guards at Mecklenburg, as it was habit acquired from the perspective that they deemed it feasible not to show partiality, and that they were capable of being just as, or more brutal, to us than their white counter parts. Whenever a prisoner was attacked by the guards, the black guards were always the assailants who had to be restrained, foaming at the mouth, bug-eyed, with the rapacity of wild beasts. They would not commit this type viciousness upon a white prisoner unless he was a familiar, hard core convict.

In the early 1970's several groups of Virginia Prisoners filed petitions in Federal courts concerning the racism of the guards. They argued that since all of the guards were white, this enhanced the monstrous racism which threatened to engulf the total system. They also reasoned that they would feel more compatible with black guards, and that their employment within the prison system would enormously diminish the racial tension between black prisoners and white guards.

Incredibly, a Federal judge ruled in their favor. A few months after this monumental ruling came in effect, there were considerable complaints from black prisoners concerning the additional brutality of the black guards. There were only ten black guards at this stage, but they were wreaking havoc wherever they were assigned to work. More black prisoners were being placed in solitary confinement with bandages on their heads, concealing stitches and gashes. Prison hospitals were suddenly overcrowded with black prisoners suffering from broken bones and open wounds.

This endless cycle of evil was considered meritorious by the administrators. They became enthusiastic about the idea of hiring extra black guards. The black principals of these brutalities were soon singled out and elevated to higher ranks. Within three years, the black guards outnumbered the white guards at least three to one throughout the Virginia prison system. This was one court victory that black prisoners of Vir₇ginia would permanently regret.

The registered nurse with the most influence at Mecklenburg at this period was a slim, sagacious, white woman with piercing eyes. Her name was Debra Painter, and she was about twenty nine years old. Her demeanor was quiet and shy, but behind this convincing facade was the most truculent and peculiar prison nurse we'd ever encountered.

She would make her rounds to pass out medication at six in the morning and at twelve noon. Usually she would catch us in various stages of undress. Some of us began to notice how she would sneak peeks at the protuberance between our legs during each round. We discussed this issue among ourselves to assure that we were not imagining things out of some level of egotism. It was unanimous among us that she peeked only between the legs of black prisoners.

We had accepted her as just another white pervert who still believed that all black men possessed gigantic penises, until she began acting out the role that exposed her true nature and caused us to churn with discontent. In liaison with Catron and his campaign to burn out the spirit of the prisoners who were still resisting unconditional, "behavior control," this witch was present during each physical attack upon us. Seven or eight guards would enter a prisoner's cell, wrestle him to the floor and beat him senseless. While the prisoner is pinned to the floor by the guards, Nurse Painter would imperiously approach him, kneel beside him and smoothly inject him with Prolixin or Thorazine, two powerful depressants which can linger in effect for two weeks! She would wait for the automatic, spasmodic motions of the prisoner then her eyes would become glossy, her whole body would shake, and her skin would turn florid, while she roamed her hands over his body in pretense of calming him down. Ray Charles could have seen that she was receiving an abnormal, sexual delight in cruelty!

For years we observed Nurse Painter doing her thing in pod areas, hallways, etc. Several guards conversed regularly about her and used words such as sick and taciturn to describe her. She continued to swagger through the pods, and even though we retaliated against her by dashing fecal matter in her face, she remained adamant in her link to this vile activity.

We were unyieldingly repressed, but a body of people cannot be so repressed that they cannot strike back in some way. We would attack the guards with prison made blow darts, spit in their faces, sling our food trays back at them, and blast them with human waste. When people are at war, for whatever reasons, and are snared in a condition that has become prejudicial, no tactic can be discounted in battle. We were not capable of challenging them effectively; we were only trying to survive. Prison authorities used our tyro guerrilla tactics to justify feeding us bag lunches, a punishment diet of unpalatable food served in tiny paper bags. They claimed that there were strict time limitations connected to this starvation diet, but some of us remained on this diet for several weeks. We were also placed in cells without a mattress, clothes, or items for hygiene, for months.

Later in the year of 1978, Abdul "Cup Cake" Wakil and nine other convicts staged the first collective, physical revolt of Mecklenburg on the yard of Building 3. They refused to be handcuffed or leave the yard peacefully, and they demanded to see the warden about the deplorable conditions of the institution. Approximately twenty minutes later, Catron and several officers dressed in full riot gear arrived at the yard. At that moment Catron became an emotional embodiment of fascistic prison force! He ordered the "Pert Team" to storm the yard and drag the prisoners out of there. The running dogs didn't hesitate for a second; firing loads of tear gas into the yard, they rushed in wildly brandishing Billy clubs. The menacing forces arrayed against these valiant convicts were daunting, but they didn't cringe in a corner. They stood tall and engaged in the hostile encounter like men. They were defeated, but they had nothing to be ashamed of.

The sequence of this battle was ghastly: The guards continued to beat the prisoners while they were down and semi-conscious. Then they were crudely dragged from the yard and up the stairs of Building 3 by their ankles. Seven of the prisoners suffered fractured ribs and broken limbs. It was two more days after the battle before they were allowed medical treatment.

Nietzsche said that anything that doesn't kill you makes you a better man. My experience at Mecklenburg makes it difficult for me to relate to this statement. From the effects of being pushed, prodded and humiliated, too many members of our atomized society were transformed into hate filled degenerates. After a few years of Mecklenburg's chastisement, a vast number of them could be found in their cells staring at the floor, jabbering hysterically.

The perennial crescendo of noise, mounting violence, and years of scorn and abandonment, begin to unbalance my mental equilibrium. I felt like a man slowly sinking in quicksand, desperately seeking anything to grasp in order to preserve the precious air flowing through my nostrils. But in my moments of deepest despair, I could still envision groups of us rising dramatically and joining in the righteous proclamation of revolt

Day of Reckoning

*"I'm Convinced that any serious
organizing of people must carry
with it from the start a
potential threat of
revolutionary violence."*

George Jackson

In July of 1984 the convicts of Mecklenburg justifiably
felt extreme enmity towards the prison authorities. An insane
crackdown was instituted after the May 31 escape and it
produced the momentum of our unity. Maliciously tough
security precautions contributed to the "Day Of Reckoning

Human feces, urine, stale food and saliva encrusted the
walls and ceilings of every pod. The air conditioners were cut
off and the tenacious heat combined with the fetid odor, was
suffocating. Our cells had not been cleaned for weeks and
there was filth on the floor over an inch thick. Blowflies were
zooming from cell to cell in droves. Warden Townley claimed
that all of this was part of the new security measures!

Because there is such total control over the life of a prisoner, his remaining domain of freedom and self-determination, small as it may be, takes on a critically important status. The consent of power to prison administrators should for this reason carry with it the consequence of scrutiny by concerned individuals standing outside the process. Thus we frequently appealed to governor Robb and several politicians to investigate the deteriorating conditions which were now threatening to consume us all. I'm convinced that many of these letters and petitions escaped through the Mecklenburg mailroom and reached their destination. A few people responded, such as Congressman Parren J. Mitchell and attorney Alvin J. Bronstein of ACLU but redress was light years away because warden Townley proved to be equal to Catron in deviousness.

On the first of July I sent a typewritten petition to governor Robb with 22 prisoner signatures attached to it. He refused to respond. He had the power to stop the future shedding of blood however, he never actually dwelled into the violence of Mecklenburg until it blew up in his face. Often politicians, disregard what is morally right to support what is politically beneficial to themselves or their associates. Robb's rejection of our petition placed him in this category.

The overdue awakening of the Mecklenburg prison masses was detected by the authorities. They knew we were coming together and their plots no longer exhibited a touch of subtleness. On the fourth of July, the privilege of yard recreation was suddenly granted to five of us. R. Hairston, a well-known informer, who had become a dodging inmate since being stabbed by a convict at Mecklenburg, was among this group. Four guards remained inside the yard with us to apply continuous attention to our activities.

We began a four man basketball game while the guards sit on the only table out there and conversed with each other. Approximately six minutes later, Hairston staggered off the court towards the guards, and then collapsed in front of them with blood gushing from one of his eyes. The guards, with startled expressions, promptly stood up and asked us what happened. "He ran into the pole tryin' to get the rebound," we answered simultaneously.

Hairston died two days later. The four of us were placed under investigation and Building 1 was locked down with orders from the warden that we be permitted only food and five minute showers. Why four so called special security guards, only eight feet away, did not see what indeed happened to Hairston was never investigated. The reason Hairston went to the yard with four stubborn convicts became a companion in his grave.

On July 12 the prison was rocked by the first indication of the power of prisoner unity and its ability to incapacitate guard force. Prisoners from Building 5 and 3 were in recreation yards across from each other. Merely seconds after recreation begin, a tiny, seventeen year old convict named Owens, attacked one of the guards stationed inside the yard with his fists. The guard broke his club across Owens' shaved head, but it didn't seem to faze him; he continued to bang the guard's jaw with the accuracy of a prize fighter. The other guard moved in to lend aid to the guard under attack and three convicts downed him, snatched his club and began kicking and beating him with the club. Minutes later nine other guards sprinted into the yard and began to savagely beat the six prisoners with Billy clubs.

On the Building 3 yard 12 prisoners were viewing this action, clutching the fence with anger. One of these prisoners was Steve Howard, a tall, youthful giant, with a history of violent conflicts with prison guards. Standing beside him, smiling with pleasure at the beatings of the convicts, was Cpl. Marvin Spruell.

"Is it funny to you, pig?" Steve asked him, then punched him up side his steeple head, knocking him down. The rest of the prisoners, already enlivened, overpowered Spruell and the other guard. Both guards were severely punished until 13 more guards ran into the yard to help them. The convicts had broke up yard tables to use the legs as weapons and they were ready for them. Nine guards and six prisoners were injured during 75 minutes of fighting. The guards won the battle only by shooting loads of tear gas in the yard. It was a battle which the Pert Team would never forget.

Two days later, angered by the reports of the battle, Director Landon vowed to take strong disciplinary action against any prisoner, who causes violence in state prisons.

"We've tried to provide reasonable facilities, such as picnic tables in the recreational areas, for the prisoners," he said. "It's sad when they react in the way they did at Mecklenburg. We are ready to handle future violence.., that's part of the business."

He visited Mecklenburg on the thirteenth and said that he was pleased with the facility's administration. If he had known that he was less than a month away from a catastrophe, he would have hid his face and buttoned his lip.

The tough security procedures at Mecklenburg were sharply criticized by a New Jersey prison consultant hired by the state to examine conditions there. He called for improved communications, sanitation and maintenance, and an end to the prison's procedures of supervising prisoner recreation yards. He questioned the practice of putting guards in enclosed exercise yards with prisoners convicted of serious offenses.

Warden Townley didn't want to hear of it. He said that he did not believe prisoners could be adequately supervised in the yards unless guards were stationed among them. Several guards began to complain about this procedure after the July 12 battle and Townley somewhat relented, ordering radio equipped guards to be stationed outside the exercise areas whenever prisoners were allowed to use them. He said that these guards could call for help if the prisoners assault the officers positioned in the yards.

A prison spokesman told a Norfolk newspaper that Townley was revamping security procedures at Mecklenburg but was not bound to follow every recommendation in the consultant's report.

"Townley is the commander on the scene. He will implement the recommendations that are feasible and suitable for the institution," the spokesman said. Famous last words!

58 Guards from the Nottoway Correctional Center were brought to Mecklenburg for a massive shake down. They had a brief meeting with Townley and top officials before the shake down was conducted. The shake down occurred on the evening of July 26. These guards were wearing no badges and it was clear that they had received cell numbers of certain prisoners listed for special treatment. This incident was the final straw it set the stage for the weekend siege that gave us the media attention we'd been seeking for so long.

These officers walked into this world of bitterness and frayed nerves, looking for trouble. They were loud, unruly, and I know I heard the profane word "motherfucker" over one hundred times. When they came to our cells, they told us to back up and be handcuffed from behind. When the door was opened, they pulled us out of our cells, snatched our pants and underwear down, forced us to spread our legs while they anally searched us, then slung us against the tier railing. We were beaten about the head, rear and genitals if we uttered the slightest protest in regards to our property being disarranged. They destroyed our legal papers, family photographs and radios, while calling us punks and low life.

Anthony "Wild Man" Yates, a convict who was involved in the July 12 battle, suffered a broken nose, a sprained thumb, and several bruises on his forehead. Larry Winston, a mentally disturbed convict, was assaulted with a Billy club and sustained a four inch bruise on his left thigh and knots on his forehead. 26 of us were beaten by these guards and we all required medical treatment.

The American Civil Liberties Union received 30 letters from us charging the visiting guards with unprovoked abuse. An internal investigation ensued and one of the guards accused of attacking Yates argued in his defense.

"We only used the force necessary to subdue dangerous inmates. We did what we were told (by Mecklenburg authorities) and they even complimented and thanked us afterwards for the fine job we did during the shake down."

We knew his first statement was a lie, but we also knew that his statement concerning the Mecklenburg authorities was right on the money.

There were now concerted efforts by us to achieve our rights as human beings and to expose this prison to the public regardless of the consequences. The problems had reached such magnitude that attempts by the administration to keep them secret were no longer possible. Timing in all situations has to be perfect to ensure maximum impact. Realizing that all prison revolts carries with them political overtones, we also understood that an earnest uprising at this period would be most uncomfortable for governor Robb and the lethargic politicians who were sitting back and allowing these unbearable conditions to persist.

I knew that something spectacular was about to happen, and I knew it had to happen in Building 5 because we (Building 1) were on lock down. We communicated with the convicts in Building 5 through the windows, but we had to talk in complex codes that were very difficult to interpret. The administration were still allowing certain Building 5 pods to receive yard recreation. Early on the morning of August 4, at about ten o'clock, I peered through my window and noticed five convict soldiers pacing the Building 5 recreation yard. I felt a coldness seep into me as I looked at their grim faces.

"Don't worry, Tommy, everything gonna be everything in a few," a convict yelled at me from a Building 5 window.

"I hear ya," I answered, moving back from the window.

Two hours later, my conversation with "Tee" Jackson, a convict who celled next door to me, was momentarily cut off by the nasalizing sound of Paul Coomer's voice on the Building 5 public address system. He automatically had our total attention.

"This building is now under siege! We are in control now. We have nine hostages and our demands will be prepared shortly. Once again, for all of my fellow comrades, this building is under siege and everything is in order at this time."

There was an outbreak of pandemonium in our pod after Coomer signed off the air. Everyone was screaming with feelings of triumph and happiness. I stumbled to my cell window with jerky movements as if I had been touched by electricity. It was stupendous! We had been waiting for this moment it seems like a million years.

An hour later, Ahoto Mulazim, a youthful convict, came to a Building 5 window and informed me that the main participants of the uprising wanted me to prepare the list of demands. I wasted no time in typing the demands that I knew would soon be broadcasted throughout Virginia. Within the next two hours, instructions, suggestions and ideas poured from the windows of Building 1. The Pert Team outside were infuriated, but this was one tide of rebellion they could not stop, because the doors on the first floor of Building 5 had been tied back with sheets and the furniture was stacked against them.

That evening, at about three o'clock, two guards came to my cell to receive the list of demands. Coomer acquired the list of demands 15 minutes later, by lowering a sheet line out of a Building 5 window. Negotiations with the administrators and political aides were now under way. Governor Robb, contrary to some of his recent reactions to prison problems, did not involve himself personally in the crisis at this period.

Winding up a three day education conference in Minnesota and scheduled to be on a national TV news show in Washington, he decided to leave the hostage situation in the hands of his most trusted aides.

Ernest Merritte, one of the guards responsible for some of our torment, suffered multiple lacerations to the head, stab wounds to the lower rib cage, a puncture wound in the thighs and multiple contusions to the back. Another guard, Leroy Williams, suffered several bruises and multiple lacerations over most of his body. Following is a list of the hostages who were still being held:

- Officer Johnson: no visible injuries
- Officer L. Coleman: no visible injuries
- Officer J. Terry: lip injury
- Alice Clary: no visible injuries
- Officer W. Maitland: cut shoulder blade, puncture wound, having trouble breathing, bleeding at the right side of the head below his left ear
- Cpl. C. Mangum: knees bruised severely, unable to walk properly, suffering and injury to his right ear

- Officer E. Toombs: a diabetic, suffering soreness in his left arm, pain in his back, and a small cut to his left ear.

Prison officials identified Paul Coomer as the leader of the takeover, but they were no longer familiar with the secrets of our family. We were not the same prisoners whose behavior was covered by a mantle of ignorance. Coomer was the main spokesman and a leader but there were four other key leaders who were splendid strategists: Rico "Doc" Holiday, Roosevelt "Speedball" Painter, Johnny "Blood" Turner, and Ahoto Mulazim. These convict soldiers were the cream of the 32 rebellious prisoners.

Coomer requested that a statement be read over a local radio station, explaining the prisoners' grievances. At 2:15 p.m. Mecklenburg Capt. Robert Goode called WJWS in Boydton. After verifying that it was a legitimate request from Mecklenburg officials, the radio station allowed a statement to be read:

"The takeover here is a request to bring to light inept and in humane treatment of the prisoners of Mecklenburg," the statement said in part. "We, the prisoners of Building 5, hereby take the only course of action to amend these conditions here at this institution."

An hour earlier, a prison official said that 53 prisoners on the second floor of Building 5 were locked in and Surrounded and, that they could take the building back at any time, but he would not reveal what their plans were beyond continuing the negotiations.

The Robb administration coordinated its response to the incident from the Corrections Department headquarters in Richmond. Director Landon was there, joined by three of Robb's top assistants: David K. McCloud, his chief of staff; Franklin E. White, a secretary of public safety and transportation; and White's deputy and soon to be new department director, Allyn R. Sielaff.

I initially prepared a list of 15 demands, and prison negotiators agreed to air them on Richmond TV stations. That list was later revised by a few leaders of the revolt to include an amnesty provision for those participating in the takeover, as well as added demands regarding treatment of visitors.

ACLU attorneys, Alvin L. Bronstein and Elizabeth Alexander, arrived at Mecklenburg shortly after 10:p.m. to assist prison officials in negotiations. Director Landon publicized two of the prisoners' demands which merited immediate attention. "One was to put the list of demands on television. The other was they wanted to talk to Bronstein."

Bronstein informed prison administrators that the prisoners would release Officer Toombs in exchange for the promise to publicize the new demands and bring ice water to them. At 10:55 p.m. Bronstein, accompanied by Ms. Alexander, was escorted by Captain Goode to the North west side of Building 5 to talk to Coomer. Captain Goode said that four prisoners talked with the attorneys. They threw a list of demands out of the window to the attorneys, and told Bronstein that they wanted the demands given to the press immediately. They wanted the water turned back on and they stated that they would discuss releasing the hostages, but not before daylight. Bronstein and Ms. Alexander asked them to allow Officer Toombs to come out, but they said, "No;" however, if the demands were given to the press and the water turned back on, they would consider releasing him.

Captain Goode escorted Bronstein and Ms. Alexander back to Building 5 at 12:40 a.m. for the purpose of telling the prisoners what the administration would agree to. They agreed to give the demands to the press, but would not agree to turn the water back on. They did agree to send drinking water to them. The prisoners said, if they heard their demands on the *news* media and if Bronstein would sample the drinking water sent to them, they would release Officer Toombs. They also said that they would not allow any more hostages to be released, nor would they do anything else until daylight; Coomer made it known that if an attempt was made to rescue the hostages, they would be killed.

"They have agreed nothing else will happen tonight, "Bronstein said. "In the morning, the prisoners will come out unarmed with the other hostages. They agreed to turn over the hostages if the act was witnessed by me, another ACLU official and media representatives."

None of the convicts in Building I attempted to sleep. During the night we all underwent hours of mental unrest hoping that the various goon squads stationed outside would not storm Building 5 and kill them all. Who could forget, Attica?

Every half an. hour, Rico or Ahoto would call to assure me that they still had the situation under control. They had the best fighters holding post at central sections of the building. There were a few problems with the different opinions of strategy and the protection of Ms. Clary from sexual assault, but they were determined to keep their unity intact.

Edwin Toombs, a guard suffering badly from diabetes, was released by the prisoners at 1:30 Sunday morning. He was interviewed by special agents immediately after his release. This interview was continued about ten minutes later at the South Hill hospital. He was interviewed again on August 6 by special agent McDowell. The impartment of this interview exposed greater details of the first interview:

Officers Williams, Coleman, and Toombs took four prisoners from the left side of C-Pod to recreation at 9:15 a.m. They were returned to their cells at approximately 10:30 a.m. The right side was handcuffed and ready to go to recreation when they returned the four to the left side. Toombs identified the following prisoners that went to the yard: Paul Coomer, James Ford, Richard Baker, N. Terry, and J. Turner. While at recreation, Officer Coleman was outside the fence with a radio and Toombs and Williams were inside with the prisoners.

After recreation was completed at approximately 11:45 a.m., the prisoners were handcuffed. Williams and Coleman were in front of the prisoners and Toombs was in the rear. At this point they were not searched, but would have been prior to being placed in the cells. Toombs left the Control Room key with the A-Control Room attendant.

Corporal Merritte was manning the Control Room of A-Pod and he let them in from the stairway. Merritte was talking on the telephone when he let them through the door. When they were walking down the corridor, convict Caffee was standing in the corridor. When they turned the corner to go toward C-Pod, Toombs didn't see anyone in B-Control Room. As Toombs turned the corner going toward the C-Pod Control Room, convict Ford got behind him and struck him in the back, knocking him to the floor. At this time, Coomer knelt down on the floor and held a homemade knife to his stomach. Coomer told him, "If you lay still, you won't get hurt." Ford took his uniform off and cuffed him with Coomer's handcuffs. He had a ring of handcuff keys in his pocket and they fell out of his pants pocket when he took his pants off. Ford then took him to cell 63. When they passed C-Control Room, he didn't see anyone inside and couldn't remember if the door was open or shut. Officer Coleman was handcuffed to the grid bars on the left side of C-Pod.

Toombs remained in cell 63 for 30 to 45 minutes, then he was taken out of cell 63 and taken to the unit office where officers Terry, Coleman, Johnson, and Cpl. Mangum were. After a short time he was taken to B-Pod and placed in a chair facing the "B" stair way door. He remembered hearing some of the prisoners say this was done in case the officers tried to rush the building, they could see the prisoners had a hostage. While in the hallway, one of the prisoners told Blood Turner that other prisoners were trying to rape Ms. Clary in C-Pod. Turner, Mulazim, and a few others took off toward C-Pod and brought Ms. Clary to the unit office. Ms. Clary was wrapped in a sheet. She was placed in the unit office again at approximately 7:05 p.m.

The leaders of the revolt operated from B-Pod Control Room and later moved to A-Control Room. Coomer told him that no one was supposed to get hurt, but that Blood Turner wanted to kill.

Coomer also told Toombs that if it hadn't been for what happened last Thursday, (July 26, 1994) the uprising would not have occurred. He said he wasn't working on the 26th, but was told that officers from Nottoway came to Building 1 and 5 and "busted ass."

At 10:30 p.m. the hostages were removed from the unit office to the counselor's office. This move was made so the injured would be more comfortable in the air conditioned office.

Corporal Merritte and Officer Maitland were put in cell 45. They were not handcuffed and the cell was not locked. Coomer and Blood Turner sent someone to get them out of cell 45. They were taken to a day room area of B-Pod and told to sit down. They then were told to lie down and they were doing so when convict Sutherland was released from his cell.

Sutherland came running out of his cell toward them saying, "You motherfucker, I'm going to kill you." Sutherland then stabbed Corporal Merritte three times and then stabbed Officer Maitland. Maitland was lying on the floor in the day room area of B-Pod near the rail on the left side of the steps. Merritte was lying on the floor near Maitland, but he was near the wall separating the left and right sides of B-Pod when the stabbings occurred.

Coomer talked by telephone only to Captain Goode until special agent R. Turner arrived. Coomer did not want to talk with Turner and when Turner got him on the phone he roused his anger by uttering threatening statements. Turner calmed him down a bit and Coomer eventually began to talk with him. It was revealed to Coomer that a 7 a.m. ultimatum had been issued by governor Robb and that state police and corrections officers were prepared to storm the building if this ultimatum wasn't met.

The ultimatum caused internal disruption in Building 5. Coomer and Blood Turner's relationship was strained by conflicting ideas regarding surrender and the treatment of the hostages. Blood rejected any type compromise with the prison administration; he felt that Coomer shouldn't have the power to make the ultimate decision (to surrender) alone. The convicts who were making the major decisions held a brief conference but the situation was almost out of hand. Blood was not the only one who wanted to take it to the max.

At 6:10 a.m. Bronstein arrived back at the window of Building 5 and began talking to Rico. He indicated that he had read the statement to the press and talked with them a number of times. Rico seemed agitated as he inquired about the lack of news coverage. Bronstein assured him that it would be in the Sunday newspapers as well as the Washington, D. C. TV station and newspapers.

Rico then informed Bronstein that the participants of the siege were losing trust in him (Bronstein) and that if he was not sincere, there was no use of anything. Rico then angrily said "The brothers don't want anything at this time but proper media exposure. I have a whole lot of killers running around, and I'm doing all I can do to keep them cool."

"Rico, don't worry... you will see it on TV soon."

"The comrades want to see it before they come out, Mr. Bronstein.?

"Rico, there are no news programs on the TV on Sunday morning." Bronstein made one more empty promise and left.

The convicts of Building 5 never received media coverage at the appropriate time, nor were there any news reporters at the scene when the hostages were released. Bronstein was lying through his teeth to the leaders because he had been advised hours earlier by ranking officials that the demand for news reporters at the scene during surrender would not be met.

At 6:26 a.m. warden Townley informed Bronstein that the following instructions were to be given to the revolting prisoners:

1. That they exit Building 5 down the back of B-Pod and onto the platform in the rear of the kitchen.
2. The hostages are to be in front.
3. The prisoners are to stay on the ramp.
4. The reporters will be present to review this at 6:30 a.m.

Blood and the convicts who supported him were voted against. Blood was discomposed; he would hold a grudge against Coomer for a long time. A number of foul comments were made about Blood in the following months, but no one could deny that he was a free spirit with a heart as wild and untamed as a windstorm. He was one of the many convicts that needed direction and discipline, but even without it, he struck terror in the hearts of the prison tyrants.

Coomer began negotiating for their safety during the release of the hostages. He called Sargent Watson and the list of instructions from warden Townley was read to him. Coomer told Watson that the hostages would be mixed among them and that is the only way they would do it. He further demanded that the ACLU lawyers and news reporters be present. He said they would not be armed and they would come out of B-Pod.

Coomer's latest call was to Sargent Handy. Minutes later Sargent Handy discussed Coomer's demands with corrections personnel. He informed them that the prisoners must not be harmed when they came out, and they must release the hostages when they reach the ramp.

Approximately 200 high strung corrections officers and state police with police dogs had moved toward Building 5 at 7 a.m. The rebels didn't come out at exactly 7 a.m. The dogs were barking non-stop, and the shotguns cuddled in the arms of the state police glistened under the blaze of the sun.

Suddenly at 7:15 a.m., after a 19 hour standoff, the door to B-Pod opened; Ms. Clary, Maitland and the other hostages stepped out. Close behind them were Coomer, Blood, Rico and Ahoto. Officers Maitland and Mangum appeared to be in very bad shape. Ms. Clary and the rest looked shaken but well physically. All of the convicts stepped out proud and expressionless. News reporters were not at the scene as they wished but their mission was accomplished.

Several ambulances were waiting to take the hostages to the hospital and two large buses were backed up to the building to transfer the 32 prisoners to C-Building in Richmond. They were loaded into the bus in twos while the police dogs growled and struggled to brake from their restraints.

"Hey, Hashim", Eugene "Speedy" Smith hollered at me. "It's something in the Sunday morning papers about you. Make sure you check it out."

"Hashim... I'll get to ya as soon as I can, stick man," came from Rico.

"Those pigs are trying to link you as a leader of this thing, Hashim, but I will straighten it. You know you will have to watch your back 'cause they gone push a thing," came from Coomer.

"Hold the fort down, Hashim," came from Ahoto.

"See ya at the next battlefield, Shim," came from Blood.

Other comrades issued revolutionary greetings and slogans as the buses eased from the building. I felt good! I felt extraordinarily good, because I knew that this revolt was the turning point; it would change Mecklenburg forever.

Two weeks before the uprising I sent identical letters relating to our predicament to the Virginia Pilot in Norfolk and the Richmond Times Dispatch. The Virginia Pilot published it on July 20. Times Dispatch never acknowledged it. Times Dispatch did publish it on the morning of August 5, which was much too late. Following is the complete text of the letter as it was published:

It has been axiomatic among us prisoners within this oppressive and brutal institution (Mecklenburg Corr. Center) that we had to venture into all types of endeavors to bring certain truths to the public. So many negative images of us are produced based upon the one sided propaganda of the state they have perpetrated this for years, and by doing so, have kept us powerless in voicing the reality of the extremely dangerous atmosphere here.

Years of silence, on our part has only been more damaging to us. Therefore I'm taking this opportunity to speak out against the dire propaganda of the state and reveal the problems and their roots from the eyes of the convicts here, and I will not issue distortions just to draw sympathy from the public as the state has done. The situation here concerns society as well as the prisoners or guards, because in the future a lot of these mistreated prisoners will be back out there with bustling hatred and a compelling desire for vengeance.

This institution was designed for the so called hard core convicts; prisoners whom the state considered unmanageable at other institutions. In 1977 the top officials here used this fact to apply illegal brute force and life threatening tactics to maintain control. They treated the prisoners like animals, and when the prisoners became violent out of anger, frustration and helplessness, they immediately crushed them with their riot teams. Society just smiled and went about their business, because they were duped to believe that prisoners are not human, have no proper values or potentials to one day live a meaningful and productive life. And violence escalated from one situation to the next.

ACLU stepped in and took the institution to court for inhumane treatment. They didn't ask for any special favors, just for the ranking officials to follow the rules as they were documented. A Federal judge deemed ACLU's suit to be within reason, and they achieved an out of court settlement, wherein the ranking officials here agreed to take most of the viciousness and injustice out of the system. They never followed through with their agreement.

Since the escape of six death row prisoners here, the guards, under direct orders of the new warden and chief of security, have committed outrageous violence and harassment against Mecklenburg prisoners, focusing their attention mainly on those in Building 1, where the escape took place. Prisoners throughout this institution are being denied all legal rights according to institutional guidelines. They are being pushed into a corner, and this will inevitably create but one result. We are forced to endure this type harassment, for situations we haven't created nor have any knowledge of.

The truth is, and history proves this, violence can only breed more violence. We are men here, regardless of what the officials say or what society thinks of us, and we stand firm and tall from this civilized perspective. Nothing positive can be produced from a situation, where human beings are being demoralized and treated like dogs.

Before too long society will have another Attica on their hands right here in Virginia. Robert M. Landon has made several foolish and unprofessional statements regarding this particular prison. He has proven, along with the rest of the state, that he's only concerned about his image and the political aspects of the situation.

The Virginia Pilot's August 5 headlines announced: Prisoner's Letter Warned of Uprising. The article described my history and the strongest appeals of the letter:

Thomas Edward Cox, 36, one of the prisoners believed to have master minded Saturday's uprising at the Mecklenburg Correctional Center, warned in a July 20th letter published in the Virginia Pilot that "before long society will have another Attica on its hands right here in Virginia."

Cox, who is serving a 66 year sentence, was convicted in 1981 for his role in the 1980 robbery and shooting in Norfolk of a Navy man. He had charged in the letter that since the recent escape of six death row prisoners, guards and prison officials "have perpetrated outrageous violence and harassment against the prisoners."

He said prisoners were "being denied legal rights," and he went on to issue a stern warning: "History proves that violence can only breed more violence."

References to "legal rights" and "institution guidelines" in Cox's letter are similar to the first item on the typewritten list of demands that Cox gave to prison officials after the uprising. It called for a "complete and logical investigation into the reason prisoners have been denied legal and institutional rights."

These are the other demands issued by Cox in behalf of the prisoners:

Immediate halt to brutal treatment from prison officials,

Proper medical treatment,

Removal of present prison officials,

Immediate halt to special treatment of punishing prisoners for acts committed by others,

Immediate halt to special punishment for suspected convict leaders,

Removal of prison officials on Institutional Classification Committee,

A modernized education system in the prison,

Increased phone and library privileges,

Immediate halt to harassment of death row prisoners,

Have all corrections officials educated to the needs of prisoners,

Sufficient hours for recreation,

Better quality of food and its preparation,

More fruit and less pork,

30 day maximum segregation for any one offense,

removal of all untrained mailroom officers.

One of the new demands included by the prisoners insisted that a previous lawsuit filed by the ACLU against Mecklenburg prison officials be reinstated. They demanded also that the current prison physician be removed, that lawyers have full access to the facility, that harassment of visitors be stopped, that visitors be allowed to smoke in the visiting room, that vending machines be installed in that room and that prisoners be allowed to take photographs with members of their families in the visiting room.

Cox and three other people were arrested by Norfolk police Dec. 17, 1980, the day after George Pollard was shot and robbed with another man while sitting in a car at Lincoln and Nicholson streets in Young Park. A fifth person was also charged later. Cox was convicted of malicious wounding, conspiracy and robbery.

In 1969, Cox and another man were charged with the armed robbery of a Virginia Beach grocery store. During the holdup, the store owner shot Cox twice in the abdomen. Cox, who was 21 at the time, was sentenced to 16 years in prison.

His father, Thomas E. Cox Sr. of Norfolk, was unaware of his son's role in Saturday's uprising. While he said he was shocked that his son had taken part, he said he was not surprised that there had been a revolt.

"I believe in law and order," he said, adding that he knew his son had done wrong and had to be punished. "He deserved it," the elder Cox said. "But I also believe you gotta give a little bit to get a little. You can't keep pushing people and pushing people. They'll push back."

The senior Cox charged that prison officials had brought on the latest troubles because they treat prisoners and prisoners' relatives and friends "like dogs."

Cox said that his son has "reason for a grievance," and he went on to cite instances of what he considers unwarranted actions by prison officials. For instance, he recalled being five minutes late recently for a scheduled visit with his son. "I drove all that distance from Norfolk, and they wouldn't let me see my son," he said. "You wouldn't treat a dog that way."

Another time, he said, he sent a commercial money order to his son only to have it refused by the prison because it was not a U.S. Postal Service money order. "By the time the new one was sent, it was too late for what my son wanted it for."

I knew without a doubt that Mecklenburg's honeymoon was over when news of the uprising produced angry reactions from legislators. Several known lawmakers said governor Robb should conduct an immediate review of the Corrections Department's top management, including director Landon. Senator Howard P. Anderson, said governor Robb should hire a consultant or a prison official from another state to revamp security and procedures at Mecklenburg. "Something is radically wrong there," said Anderson, who was chairman of the Senate subcommittee that visited the prison in late July. "Expertise which is not there now has to be brought in."

On August 10th, Sgt. Chris Gibb and Lt. Mike Rea, were fired for allegedly beating prisoners Yates and Winston. The heat was on! Both guards denied using excessive force and they predicted more uprisings at the prison.

"We only used the force necessary to subdue dangerous prisoners; we did what we were told," asserted Lt. Rea.

"I'm disgusted and disappointed; we're being used as scapegoats," said Sgt. Gibbs.

Rea and Gibbs accused prison officials and governor Robb of making them the political fall guys for the state's most troubled prison. Both vowed to fight the firings through the state's grievance system.

"We're not going down by ourselves," Rea said. "We're two dead bones being thrown to the dogs because of the political climate."

They argued that it was outrageous for governor Robb and director Landon "to talk tough about dealing with these mean prisoners" and then turn around and blame last week's taking of nine hostages at Mecklenburg on excessive force used by the officers during the July 26 shake down.

Rea said that Mecklenburg's new security chief, Capt. Herb Bryant, told them that morning, "If there's any bleeding, I don't want it to be correctional officials."

"It was just like walking into a garbage dump infested with attack dogs," Gibbs said. Rea described the conditions in the two buildings searched as "Like a picture from Dante's Inferno," where the warden had warned them some prisoners would be armed and had recently assaulted guards.

Gibbs and Rea said that prisoners were "completely crazy," which was a lie to justify their actions. They also said that human waste and food was sticking to the walls of the cellblocks that reeked of urine and thick smoke from burning mattresses.

A day later, Allyn Sielaff, deputy secretary of transportation and public safety, called for both prisoners and officers to "cool down" and "restore a normal climate." "Otherwise people are going to continue to get hurt and neither the officers nor the prisoners want that," he said.

The violent uprising stemmed, in part, from the actions of the 58 outside guards who participated in the vicious shake down of July 26, but every veteran Mecklenburg official knew that it was the sequence of years of mental and physical abuse. Several news reports misled the public into believing that 32 prisoners risked their lives and release dates because of one incident.

But all of the truth could not be suppressed. A Richmond Times Dispatch article proved it with this report:

The design and behavior modification program at Mecklenburg Correctional Center provoked the disturbances and taking of hostages at the rural prison, a Board of Corrections investigative panel was told in a closed session.

"I have consistently said that a behavior modification institution like Mecklenburg cannot work even under the best of circumstances and they certainly don't exist there," Chan Kendrick said in an interview.

Kendrick said he provided that diagnosis of the continuing imbroglio surrounding the 300 convict prison during a 90 minute appearance before the corrections subcommittee. His cure for Mecklenburg's problems, Kendrick said he explained in his appearance, is to "turn it into another maximum security prison. The prison still has a phased system that's punitive in nature and based on fear on the parts of the guards, staff and prisoners."

Kendrick stated further that the ACLU won what it considers major concessions from the state prison system more than a year ago when the state agreed to change some programs and operations at the prison. The ACLU had sued the state in Federal court, but the state and the ACLU agreed to settle it before it came to trial. Despite that court approved settlement, Kendrick said that behavior modification, under which prisoners are granted privileges based on their actions, is still the central operating philosophy at the prison.

State police seemed obsessed with the issue of ex-hostage Alice Clary. She was white and most of the 32 participants of the uprising were black. For some reason they were convinced that she had been raped and was reluctant to reveal it. From several newspaper accounts, there were also many white Virginias interested in this subject.

Ms. Clary was interviewed by state police at the hospital on August 6, and again on August 8 at her residence. She stated in the first and second interview that she was not sexually molested while being held hostage at Mecklenburg Corr. Center. She stated that the only injury she suffered was when she was struck on the side of her face. She said she did not know who tore her clothes off. When asked about the blood being on her underclothes when they were found, she said she observed a prisoner wipe blood off his shoes with them.

She said that while talking on the telephone in the hallway of Building 5, she turned around and saw ten or twelve black prisoners coming up the hall from B-pod going toward A-pod. They all had either night sticks, shanks, or broken chair legs. One prisoner yelled to her to get the motherfucking phone hung up, then someone hit her on the left side of her face.

After she was taken hostage, she was carried to cell 34, which was on the left side of B-pod. On the way to the cell, several of the prisoners told her they were going to rape her. When they put her in the cell, some of the prisoners tore her clothes off. They took her apron to gag her mouth and tied her hands with a sheet behind her back. After she was bound, they made her lie down on the bed and she was covered with a sheet. The prisoner in the cell told her he would not let anyone hurt her.

While she was in cell 34, she could see the prisoners breaking up the furniture and destroying other items. Several other prisoners came into the cell and told her they were going to fuck her, but the prisoner in the cell told them to leave her alone.

She was in the cell about two hours before two black prisoners came and removed the gag from her mouth. They untied her hands but handcuffed them harder behind her. One prisoner wanted to know where her clothes were and she told him they were on the floor. He unlocked one of the handcuffs and allowed her to put her clothes back on. She was then taken to cell 40 on the left side of B-pod. The prisoner in this cell was known as "Shorty." He was crying and said he was not involved but was only doing what he was told because he was scared.

The black slave did not ravish the white mistress. The supreme scandal of white honor could not be produced.

The August 4 uprising led to the removal of warden Sherman Townly, chief of security Herbert Bryant and director Robert Landon. There were wide ranging recommendations to upgrade the conditions at Mecklenburg, and the behavior modification phase system was dismantled; but it was a hollow victory for us because the demand for an amnesty provision for those who participated in the takeover was not met, the Pert Team was still intact, and Mecklenburg was still an unremorseful monster of idleness and violence.

The Brileys Are Executed

"Now what a state of society is that which knows of no better instrument for its own defense than the hangman, and which proclaims, through the "leading journal of the world," its own brutality as eternal law?"

   Karl Marx

Three weeks after the uprising I was transferred to C-Building. I was relieved to be away from Mecklenburg and closer to the convict soldiers. The Mecklenburg Chairman of Classification, W. Crenshaw, sent a memo with me to the C-Building Classification Committee, which stated that Mecklenburg authorities recommended that I not be housed close to Paul Coomer, because we were the leaders who concocted the August 4-5 uprising and conspired for its success. This assumption was absurd, but understandable because the Mecklenburg regime's death throes were annihilating all of its limited rational.

JB, Linwood, and the other four escapees were still housed in the basement of the State Penitentiary. Late in September, Linwood was put on death watch, a situation placing a condemned prisoner under unbroken scrutiny until he is executed by the state. Under the conditions of death watch, no other prisoner is allowed to be anywhere near the condemned prisoner. When the guards entered the basement to enforce this rule by removing JB and the others, JB bucked, refusing to leave his brother alone. He resisted valiantly; the guard force shot him at close range with a stun gun and subdued him. He then was shipped with the others to the basement of M-Building at the State Farm.

U.S. District Judge D. Warriner denied Linwood's appeal for a stay of execution and review of his case on October 2. Most of us were under the impression that the state was out for personal revenge against Linwood and that nothing on God's earth could now save him. Judge Warriner's decision came in the second of two appeals on Linwood's behalf that were moving through the Federal court system as his execution date, October 12, approached.

In the appeal before Judge Warriner, Linwood's lawyers charged that he was denied a fair trial because of jury selection procedures. They attacked the exclusion from the pool of potential jurors opposed to capital punishment, even when those jurors could fairly decide Linwood's guilt or innocence. They also charged that the Virginia death row penalty statute was applied in a discriminatory manner. Statistics show that people who kill white victims are more likely to be sentenced to death than people who kill nonwhites, the lawyer said.

"This particular case has been reviewed and the conviction and sentence confirmed repeatedly" Judge Warriner responded. "The amassed weight of all of these judgments by all of these judges renders almost, if not quite, frivolous an argument that Briley has been denied fundamental fairness."

The first week in October, I received letters from several comrades in M-Building, advising me that JB was taking the situation with his brother uncharacteristically hard. He would not talk to anyone and he was barely eating. I, like most of us, did not want the execution to take place, but I faced reality and accepted Linwood as a dead man.

Two nights before the scheduled execution, C-Building was silent. Convicts paced their cells languidly and statements were limited to seven or eight words; the most popular was: "Man, have you heard anything on the news?"

An hour before the execution on October 12 the guards were afraid to walk the tiers. The suppressed hatred of authority had quietly surfaced among the convicts; the guards knew this was a period for cautiousness. We were all now waiting, some hoping for a stay of execution, others praying for his death.

From news reports we learned that the murderous side of humanity in Virginia had soared during the night of October 12. Hordes of crowds accumulated at the prison, mostly whites, chanting, "Fry the nigger,"

The radio newscaster announced at 11 o'clock that Linwood was dead. The news was followed by angry curses, mumblings, and personal radios being slammed to the floor. I paced to my bed, sit down and stared at the wall, drained of emotion.

A few days after the execution JB sent a poem to Fysk, a State Penitentiary magazine, titled Linwood, in dedication to his brother:

"My brother Linwood was here but now he's gone

up in heaven just carrying on

Some of us sit back and cry for a man so sweet...

My brother Linwood is the guy of whom I speak.

He stood fast and strong, under a "political wrong"

A mad man a monster, is what he was called

but that was only by people who knew him not at all

They dragged me away that shoulder which to cry

so that he may suffer by himself because

he refused to just lay down and die

I spoke to my brother at 5:55 p.m. on October 12th

He was holding real strong

even though he was being done wrong

He told me he loved me which I already knew,

but to hear it straight from him it was really

something new...

I asked what I could do to help him make it through...

He asked me to remain strong and never give up the fight

If he should go down this cold dreary night

Linwood went down at 11 o'clock sharp

The call by the butchers who took away his heart...

The chair was still 'warm' from the last who set

Coppola, was his name, who wanted what he got...

Keeping his "dignity" in tack

My brother is at peace, and that I'll bet-

sitting with God, while we wonder about that

Wonder as we may it is as I say

because I had a talk with Linwood

right here yes, today

Oh, smile brother smile, you are at peace

for a long, long time..."

The last time I saw JB was in December of 1984.
During this period he was totally enveloped in the struggle
for his life through the intricacy of the Virginia judicial
system. His appeals were being denied in rapid succession;
it was obvious that the state wanted him just as dead as
Linwood. I had been transferred back to Mecklenburg
because the convict soldiers were revolting in C-Building,

and routinely I was considered a massive threat because of my dogged attempts to unify all prisoners.

I saw him sitting at the table playing cards with several men in the death row Pod as I was being escorted to the Building-1 recreation yard. He looked haggard, with dark circles under his eyes, but his innate exuberance still managed to shine when he noticed me. He was smiling as he ran to the bars and cried, "Well if it ain't the old rebel slave, Hashim Khan! What's happenin' with you, my man?"

"Nothing except the same old bullshit, bro," I answered, trying not to look startled by his shaggy appearance. "They had a little thing at C-Building, and as always, I was singled out as the instigator," I added.

"Yeah, I heard about that crap... let them tell it, you are the cause of every protest in the system. These pigs should give the brothers some kinda credit for bein' able to speak up for themselves when they are mistreated."

"JB, how do your case look?" I asked, while one of the guards tugged at my arm.

He looked serious for about three seconds, and then said: "Not too good, Shim, but it's no big deal with me anymore. I mean, I don't want to go out like that, but I know Robb is out for blood, and I won't give them any of that humble, beggin' stuff, you know what I mean?"

"1 can dig it, bro," I said, backing down the hallway with a guard holding my arm. Turning the corner and going down the steps to the yard, I heard his last words: "Give 'em hell, Hashim."

On March 28th, 1985, JB married Evangeline Redding, a freelance writer and longtime civil rights activist from Halifax, North Carolina. He was just a few days from death watch in the basement of the State Penitentiary. This was the first wedding at this site and the ceremony was carried out just steps away from the state's electric chair. JB was scheduled to die on April 18.

During the ten minute ceremony performed by a prison chaplain, JB and Ms. Redding held hands and kissed, but he had to stand inside his cell. Ms. Redding and JB's father were strip searched upon entering the prison, and 15 to 18 guards and plain clothes officials were in the cell block basement during the wedding. Minutes after the ceremony, the bride briefly argued that JB was the victim of "racist" courts and prosecutors, and she was noticeably upset about the strict security and last minute change in the ceremony which was originally set for the 29th.

In his vows, JB asked supporters to remember Linwood and said that he himself was "dying so unnecessarily from injustice and corruption."

JB's father, James Sr., said his son was "real happy." As for the wedding, "I like it, it's great. That's what he likes and it's fine with me.... what she's doing will not do any harm."

These were JB's last few moments of self-contentment.

JB was always more popular and flamboyant than Linwood, thus his execution was expected to be a more striking event than Linwood's but the administration received much more than they bargained for, because this execution propelled the first mass armed attack against State Penitentiary guards. JB had many friends and admirers in the prison system and some of them were stout hearted convict soldiers. These convicts were laying low while scheming together weeks ahead of the scheduled execution. Bobilly, Rubar Pollard, and many others were now in the State Penitentiary's main population from the results of new director A. Sielaff's dismantling of Mecklenburg as a super maximum security prison.

On April 18th I was back in C-Building after being transferred from Mecklenburg because of a minor disturbance there. I was confined to a cell in the basement where the 32 Mecklenburg insurgents were housed. There was no air circulation and the heated stench was pure hell to endure, but we were not complaining about any discomfort at this period; all of our conversations were geared to JB's scheduled execution.

Typical in the manner that prison officials underestimate convicts, they were previously warned through informants that a serious move would be made against them on April 18 in an attempt to stop JB's execution, but their heed was foolishly inappropriate. Thoughts of Linwood's unhindered execution motivated their relaxed state, but JB would prove to be a formidable rival even hours away from death.

At about 7:45 a.m., just after breakfast, the convict soldiers launched a ferocious attack against the Penitentiary guard force. The guards were not mentally prepared for the swiftness or savagery of the attack, and were not able to professionally respond. Initially four guards were attacked in B-Building, a building used by both maximum and medium security prisoners. Other guards came to their aid moments later but they were also attacked by the additional convicts who joined the melee. The guards were repetitiously stabbed and their blood painted the floor and walls of the building. Extra guards in riot gear quelled the fighting at 8 a.m. All of the prisoners were locked in their cells and prison officials began searching the institution for weapons.

Nine guards were injured; four of them needing immediate surgery. Three had been knifed in the abdomen, including Capt. J. Stroble, who was twice sent to surgery and nearly died prior to surgery. Three guards were treated for minor injuries and two others were hospitalized without the need of surgery. The convicts had made their statement.

Six hours later, I heard the voices of Bobilly and three other convicts as they were being processed for confinement to the C-Building basement. The necessary scapegoats were being rounded up and the Penitentiary informants were as loose tongued as ever.

At 3:00 p.m. JB's lawyers were still fighting for his life. They produced a surprise witness, Priscilla Scarborough, whose tearful words frequently were barely audible in the courtroom. Ms. Scarborough was a Richmond native who was serving a five year prison term in the women's prison in Goochland County. Her testimony revealed that she had dated Duncan Meekins, the state's star witness against JB, at the time of the murders. She said that Meekins had actually fired the bullets that killed a pregnant woman and her child, murders for which JB was sentenced to die. She added that she had heard rumors about the murders in the Highland Park neighborhood where she and the Brileys lived. She said Meekins denied having participated in the murders when she asked him but when she persisted, he answered that "he'd been paid to do it by some people in Washington."

"When I asked him how he could kill a baby, he said he just closed his eyes," she said.

Judge Warriner ruled that Ms. Scarborough's testimony "was not credible." Her credibility was damaged chiefly by her claim on the witness stand that she did not write a letter to JB, which the state presented at the hearing.

Moments after judge Warriner's rejection of Ms. Scarborough's testimony, JB said in a telephone interview from his cell, "I'm just trying to hang in there. If worse comes to worse, I guess I'll send it (his wedding ring) out by my attorney." He kept abreast of the legal maneuverings of his case by radio.

JB ate a last meal of fried shrimp and a soft drink at 7 p.m. An hour later he showered and guards shaved his head in the final rites of execution.

At 9 p.m. the whole event had become reminiscent of the lynch mobs of the 1920s. A group gathered in front of the prison at 8 p.m. and grew from several dozen to several hundred by 10 p.m. They were screaming obscenities and burning black effigies, while a contingent of at least two dozen uniformed officers, the police bureau's SWAT unit and two canine officers poised close to the near riotous demonstrations.

JB walked to the death chamber in the basement of the State Penitentiary shortly before 11 o'clock, just a few hours after his lawyers dropped further appeals to save him. He was smiling as he was strapped into the electric chair in view of nine witnesses in a glass enclosed room. He asked the witnesses twice, "Are you happy?"

He was electrocuted at 11:02 and pronounced dead at 11:07. It was all over... JB and Linwood were physically gone forever, and from their perspective, the state had received retribution in the only manner in which complete satisfaction could be attained.

Exile

Soon after JB's execution it was obvious that rigid attention was being focused on me by the state, and that I was now one of the targeted leaders of resistance. But time also proved that I had become the ultimate target! The seeds of resistance that sprouted in Mecklenburg took root among convicts in every major Virginia institution. Convict soldiers who had learned to hate at Mecklenburg were now confined to different institutions within the state. The number of attacks by convicts against guards increased dramatically, and they (convicts) were making the ignorant prisoners conscious, causing them to suffer more, as life is always easier for fools in prison.

It did not take long for our elation from the uprising to give way to despair while confined to the heated bowels of C-Building. We were once again confronted with oppression and inflexible oppressors who were impervious to the rightfulness of our cause. The state's vengeance arrived in a preeminent degree.

On April 24 I was sitting on my bunk, dejected with thoughts of how I could gain some perspective on my life, when Lt. Hubbard stepped to the bars of my cell and told me to pack my belongings because I was being transferred to Buckingham, a minimum security institution. I automatically rejected this information because Buckingham was not accepting prisoners with my reputation. Hubbard was prepared for my skepticism; he deceived me further by taking close to an hour to convince me that Marie Deans, a paralegal and friend of mine at the time, was on the phone and had sent word that the transfer to Buckingham was legitimate because she had talked to the Warden and he agreed that I needed a break. I fell prey to the deception and left the building peacefully to discover a Powhatan Correctional Center van waiting for me.

My anger swelled as I descended the steps to the M-Building basement; this latest deception was eating at me like a cancer. Convict soldiers were shouting my name and hitting me with inquiries but I remained silent in my rage.

Moments after entering my designated cell, I informed the guards that I would attack at the first opportunity, and that I would continue to attack until I was removed or given an explanation as to why I was being shipped from one hole to another. They cursed me out and walked away from my cell.

Two days later I threw a full cup of urine into the faces of a guard and nurse. The next day I was transferred to Mecklenburg. I remained there only 15 days before I was shipped back to C-Building. 15 days later I was shipped back to M-Building. I knew then that something was terribly wrong; this practice was abnormal even for Virginia administrators.

At Mecklenburg I filed a state grievance regarding the unreasonable series of transfers; I requested an end to them because I was being denied access to my personal funds, property, and legal aid. The grievance officer's report quickly solved the mystery of my situation: "The Regional Administrator's policy of transferring you every 15 days stems from your negative leadership and the fact that this leadership has caused turmoil at several institutions. These transfers are necessary to limit your ability to establish a power base at any one institution."

During the frequent transfers I was called several times to testify at the trials of a few convicts who were involved in the Mecklenburg uprising. I went out of my way to inform the public, through my testimonies, what really happened and why the revolt occurred. I knew I was a marked man and could lose nothing in my attempts to inform the public that depends upon accurate reports. I also knew that the state would have to do something with me before 1986; perhaps assassinate me, as is usually the case in these situations.

This latest attempt to silence me by transferring me from one hole to another, every 15 days, began to take its toll. I contacted a Richmond lawyer, Gerald Zerkin, and explained my predicament to him. Several days later, with added information from Marie Deans, Zerkin sent a straight to the point letter to the Director of adult Services:

Dear Mr. Murray:

I have been contacted by concerning the unusual series of transfers to which he has been subjected. Mr. Cox has been transferred six times since April 24, 1985, each time being transferred within 15 days. During this time,

Mr. Cox never received a charge and has never appeared before the I. C. C.

While we are both well aware that the department is free to transfer inmates at will, I believe a strong argument can be made that the department cannot transfer in this fashion to avoid due process requirements, nor can it endlessly transfer an inmate regardless of its motives.

It goes without saying that Mr. Cox is disturbed by his treatment since April 24. His personal property can't keep up with him and no one knows where to visit him from one day to another. After nearly three months, it's time for the department to decide what it's going to do with him. I would appreciate your looking into this matter as soon as possible.

During my meeting with Mr. Cox on July 8, he advised me that, at the time of his first transfer from the Penitentiary Lt. Hubbard had told him that Marie Deans, who was assisting me in this matter as my paralegal was on the phone and had said it was alright for him to go. Although Lt: Hubbard denied any knowledge of this incident, I do not take his denial very seriously for several reasons. First, he continually tried to change the subject. Second, he said that "some of them may have told him that to get him to go." Third, his denial was less then emphatic.

While I recognize that officers may find it expedient to trick inmates into cooperating, this interference in the attorney client relationship is intolerable and represents yet another example of the lack of respect which many employees of the department have for the integrity of that relationship. I consider this a serious episode and one which indicates that the department's personnel are in need of some education on the subject of the attorney client relationship.

I look forward to hearing from you or your designee as to Mr. Cox's status.

Sincerely,

Gerald T. Zerkin

This letter forced the prison official's hand and enhanced their desire to get rid of me. A week later the Director of Adult Services terminated the revolving transfers, but he never mentioned what they had in store for me. The spirit of their vengeance would not die so easily.

C-Building finally blew up on July 24. I immediately outlined our many complaints in a petition to Michael Samberg, the Penitentiary Warden. Samberg and several officials talked with me and three leaders of the Mecklenburg uprising but nothing was resolved. Each official stared at me as if I was an endangered species.

For approximately 12 hours, screaming convicts set clothes and other materials on fire, threw the burning material on walkways outside their cells, broke toilets and other property, flooded their cells and used razor sharp broken porcelain pieces' to pelt prison officials who attempted to put out the fires. Amid the smell of smoke and the near deafening shouts of enraged convicts, four five man shakedown teams equipped with helmets, riot clubs and stun guns, searched us and our cells. Our unity was uncontrollable and, as was becoming a trend, the administration felt that this unity was sustained by the efforts of one man.

The next day I was escorted to a tiny room to meet with three officials and the Penitentiary's spokeswoman. The spokeswoman was conducting the meeting; she straightforwardly asked me why I was leading a revolt at C-Building. I denied this and stated that I was only attempting to voice our complaints articulately. She said there was information that I was giving instructions through the window to the prisoners upstairs, and then she asked me if I would get them to stop. I told her that I did not have that kind of power. Another official interrupted and sarcastically said that everywhere they put me, even for short periods, there are revolts by prisoners. I left this meeting with the strangest feeling; I knew the state was about to make its move.

Five days later, water stood on the cellblock floor amid food, plates, mattress stuffing, and broken toilets amid other debris. Water swept out from cells above spilled onto the floor to add to the mess. A C-Building case worker made his way through all of this to walk to the bars of my cell and hand me an Interstate Corrections Compact Form. "Well Tommy," he said, "I guess you have been expecting this."

I began to read the first paragraph: This is to inform you that, pursuant to the provisions of the Interstate Corrections Compact, as provided under Sections 53-304.9 and 53-304.

10. Code of Virginia, Acts of 1977, you are currently being considered for an involuntary transfer to the State of New Mexico ...... for the following reasons (s).

Documented adjustment history and inability to be placed in a general population in the Division of Adult Institutions in Virginia

I was stupefied as I looked up at the case worker and asked him, "Can they really do this and get away with it?"

"Tommy, from what I gather, these people are desperate in getting you out of their hair, and I think they are going to pull this one off," he answered.

I called my lawyer that night and he informed me that he and Ms. Deans would be at the committee hearing to aid me in stopping the transfer. We found out before the hearing that the deck was stacked against me because the new Director of Virginia Corrections was, against due process, ordering the transfer.

My first hearing was convened on August 6, which was adjourned by the hearing officer due to the failure to provide me with any reasons for the proposed transfer. Another hearing was commenced on August 9, and even with the emphatic and valid arguments of Mr. Zerkin, the

176

committee recommended my transfer to New Mexico at the conclusion of the hearing. The Director approved the proposed transfer the same day; their vengeance was swift and complete.

Soon after the last committee hearing, Mr. Zerkin filed an action for injunctive relief in my behalf, alleging that the Director was about to violate my right to be free from cruel and unusual punishment, mainly by sending me such a distance from relatives and friends to a prison system that has had a recent history of extreme racial violence and turmoil. This action further stated that approximately 40% of the prison population of the state's only maximum security institution was in protective custody (it was common knowledge that the institution spoken of was particularly dangerous for black prisoners and essentially beyond the control of its administrators.)

A hearing was commenced a day later in Federal court; Zerkin conducted a telephone interview with the Warden of the New Mexico prison, and he convinced the judge that conditions there had changed positively for black prisoners; he emphasized that I would have no serious problems there because of the color of my skin. The judge stated that he would make a ruling on my case at a later date.

Two days later the Richmond Times Dispatch announced that a Federal judge refused yesterday to block the transfer of a State Penitentiary inmate to the New Mexico prison system despite the inmate's contention that the move would violate his constitutional rights. It further stated that ", an inmate state, authorities have described as troublesome, requested the temporary restraining order, which was denied by U.S. District Judge Robert R. Merhige Jr."

I called several family members that night and informed them that, like the era of slavery, I was being transferred hundreds of miles away with no consideration given to my needs, feelings or resources. This was difficult for them to accept or comprehend, but the cruelty of prison rulers has always been immune to the pain of prisoners' families.

At 4 a.m. on August 21, the date of George Jackson's assassination, over a dozen prison guards escorted me out of C-Building to the basement of the Penitentiary's death row. Four hours later, refusing to give me my daughter's picture or any of my property, they turned me over to two Federal Marshalls. I was taken by van to Pennsylvania, and then flown to Oklahoma two days later. After residing in the Oklahoma jail for two weeks, I was taken by bus to an Oklahoma Federal Penitentiary called El Reno. The next day I was taken by bus to another Federal Penitentiary in Texas called La Tuna. I was driven by car to a women's prison in Grants New Mexico a week later. This is the receiving unit for male New Mexico prisoners; I remained there for 30 days.

In October I finally arrived at the State Penitentiary of New Mexico, a prison where blacks are an unpopular minority. It is a heinous society of guard corruption, racism, narcotic abuse, homosexuality, and mind boggling prisoner on prisoner violence.

The most dreadful thing for me was being surrounded by apolitical prisoners. A revolutionary, whose ideas have no force or effect, is like a bird with no wings. I was confined only to maximum security units; the only contact I had with my family derived through letters and infrequent phone calls.

I believe the violent attitude against blacks by other non-blacks was the reason I was sent there, coupled with the fact that my organizing skills were null in such a racist environment. Life was harder than it had ever been for me in prison, but the Virginia prison system had already made me a very hard man.

Prior to being shipped to the State of Connecticut, where I am confined today, for three tempestuous years I was threatened, set up numerous times to be attacked in the law library, had human waste thrown in my cell, etc. I survived because after a while in places like this, you thrive from adversity, or become a weak, useless leech, being daily used and abused by heartless guards and the many monsters in these steel cages. I prefer death to this; thus resistance is still my hope and method.

A Convicts Metamorphosis

In my lonely search for truth and understanding, I traveled many roads that led me nowhere. So many aspects of life, especially human behavior, bewildered me, and this impelled the drive that plunged me to the depths of odious activities. My personal growth elevated in stages, but there were an indefinite number of lapses, and I allowed myself to become influenced too often by astute, so called black leaders. Confusion, ignorance, and deliberate distortion of facts by these so called leaders directed my life and plagued it with destructive errors.

Through the long, bitter and cold years of confinement, several times my brain has flashed images of myself as a child; shy, gentle and inquisitive. I was also a loner and Mama's boy who abhorred violence of any type. Life was simple and sweet for me at this period; my mother was the center of my world. My ghetto environment and the need to defend myself, unsettled my gentleness and shifted me towards violence, but the fulminating violence I was later capable of committing so calmly in prison, was alien to me.

My metamorphosis, like most, has been painful and difficult, but I cherish it because it was instrumental in my total commitment to revolution, to persistent struggle for the dignity and betterment of oppressed people. The "revolutionary" is the most powerful and .conscious human being on earth. He/she is willing to change a million different times if necessary to get it right, and when he/she feels it is right only the finality of death can stop him/her, and in some cases, like Comrade George Jackson and Harriet Tubman, even then his/her ideas continue to inspire people to fight on. This fabulous way of life invented in me the compulsive urge to look inwardly for the redeeming qualities that dwells within most of us.

When I first entered prison in 1969, brainwashed, young and bursting with energy, I became a "Black Muslim" under the teachings of Mr. Elijah Muhammad. After studying the history of the European race, it was easy for me to believe that they were devils, and they were intrinsically liars and murderers. The teachings of Mr. Muhammad made me a fanatical racist who hated white people just because they were born white. I ceased the usage of profane language and stopped calling my charming African sisters "bitches." For the first time in my life I believed in something and began to practice self-discipline.

In June of 1970, I began to question three of Mr. Muhammad's theories, theories in which I was never able to fully accept. First, he taught us that a stranger appeared in Detroit in the midsummer of 1930 named Fard. We called him Master Fard. This stranger supposedly taught Mr. Muhammad. Mr. Muhammad claimed that he, above all previous prophets, had the privilege to meet God in person. Second, we were taught that (and this was the rigorous foundation of the Black Muslims) the white race was created by a black scientist with a huge head named "Yakub." Yakub supposedly discovered that the black man has two germs in him. The germs are black and brown. The brown germ is weaker than the black germ, and it can be grafted into its last stage, which is white. It was explained to us that this was the reason white people were so evil and beyond reform. The third theory I questioned was that we as Muslims, were obligated to obey any authority. This theory placed us in a stressful dilemma, and was turning many convict Muslims into submissive prisoners.

I was soon labeled a hypocrite for openly questioning these theories; subsequently I was suspended from the "Black Muslim" circle for 60 days. I feigned anger from the suspension, but deep down I was relieved because I had become disillusioned with their inactivity and robot like attitudes. I was not allowed to grow and function for the benefit of oppressed prisoners, only for members of the "Nation of Islam." I knew this was something I had to get as far away from as possible.

One ice cold night in August of 1970, I escaped from a Virginia road camp; three days later I was caught trying to jump a train, hungry, cold and filthy. Those West Virginia Mountains kicked sparks from my ass! I was sentenced to an extra year for escape and transferred to the state penitentiary in Richmond, Va. This was like going to college for me. I was surrounded by more intelligent and mature prisoners, and there were books everywhere! I was always borrowing books and debating with the rebel convicts about politics and struggle. I began to study social issues, and the concept of self-improvement was no longer considered a "chump's game" to me.

The state penitentiary was a savage, dog eat dog world at this period. No weak prisoners survived. The prisoners who entered the big yard for the first time were ogled through the lustful eyes of deadly sexual predators; they were called "booty bandits." Most of these fools had been in prison over 15 or 20 years. Many of them had been raped and mentally abused when they came in young and afraid. They had also been stabbed several times by some of their victims, and they had killed many of their victims. These were sick men with no sense of reason. I was forced to put my political education on hold; staying alive and maintaining my manhood was much more important.

Young, slender and smooth faced, I had to prove myself. I received two murder charges in 1974 for the killings of two inmates, which were later thrown out of court for lack of evidence. I grew into a complete animal; my life became a swirl of rage and violence. It was a steel jungle and I adapted very well. In this state of mind, after my release from segregation, I met some of the hardened and legendary killers like James "Piss Piss" Peterson and

George Flight. These were the most talked about prisoners in the system. They were the silent, dangerous men that no one wanted a beef with. I learned how to "stalk," master deception, and how to properly use a knife from watching and listening to these guys. At this point I wanted more than just to survive; I wanted everyone to know that I was dangerous if provoked.

I was doing 30 days in the hole in December of 1975 when a close friend sent me a book called "Soledad Brother." This book of force, a collection of letters from a self-educated, political prisoner, changed my life... I never was the same man again. I can still remember how exhilarated it left me feeling. This book exerted a potent influence on my thinking about struggle, unity, and sacrifice. George Jackson, the young black author of this book, was a self-styled revolutionary who had been in prison for ten years, seven of them in solitary confinement. He altered his negative life style in prison, began to study politics, history, philosophy, literature. He elevated the strength of his mind and body to the point that he became the most hated prisoner by the guards and the most respected and admired by the prisoners. He later was killed in a so called escape attempt by shots from a tower guard while running across the segregation yard with a gun in his hand. This just convinced me that he was for real til the end. I walked out of the hole in January, heart still cold, but determined to improve as a man and an "African revolutionary."

I began to see everything more clearly. I observed my pitiful surroundings and it was repulsive to me. The convict killers whom many prisoners feared were no longer heroes to me. What the hell did they know? They only harmed other prisoners. Only a handful confronted the prison guards or any other agents of the ruling class. I became a loner for a period, and then I began to revolt against authority in the most effective manner: organizing. I led revolts all over the system, from one dungeon to the next. I preached incessantly about black on black prison murders, our lack of unity, our lack of respect for black women, our traditional cowardice in the face of our real enemies, revolution, and the need for a prison movement that was powerful enough to make the prison administrators feel threatened.

I learned to be tolerant of other people's religious beliefs, even though I no longer believed in organized religion. I listened to people with opposing ideas and beliefs, and I respected them, but I would draw the line when these ideas and beliefs did not support the struggle in some form. I believed then as I believe now, that prisoners and black Africans in the streets have to overlook the petty things that keep us divided, we have to be compassionate towards each other's flaws, and demonstrate ceaseless unity and love and respect in order to seriously combat the ominous onslaught of oppression we daily face. In this frame of mind I was motivated to break loose from the ingrained values of not just the prison system, but the entire rotten system of America! Being a revolutionary forced me to reexamine every aspect of American and prison society, two different worlds with their own set of laws and rules for the poor and the powerless.

America was a stupendous idea that didn't work American prisons never had a chance to work. My Metamorphosis derived from the personal choices made, and I didn't want to continue to behave like the tyrants who ruled my body. Even though I continue to exist in America's "dungeons of hell," I want to feel good about myself when I look in the mirror in the morning. I want my daughter, my grandsons, and the next generation of oppressed people to feel good about me and what I have become.

In 1985, a few months before my exile to New Mexico, I began to seriously notice the actions of most of my comrades, and I began to understand what was missing within our ranks: total commitment. They were no longer paragons of brotherly behavior with each other, and they were morally depraved. As soon as they were off the battlefield and placed in a main population, they resumed the corrupt, individualistic ways of the oppressor. This rude awakening forced me to stop half stepping and commit myself totally to the struggle. If the prison officials cannot manipulate you and control your mind; if you couldn't be bought and you were not into drug or sex games, then you are a threat to them. This is the edge that I never want to lose.

Reading and studying the history of revolution and revolutionaries finally unraveled the "cloud of mystery" that had followed me most of my life. This knowledge gave me a different but positive perspective of the long and bitter struggle of my people to be free and respected in a society that's still basically racist and murderous towards them.

Revolution (in any form) offers the only hope of liberation and salvation for the oppressed people of America, in or out of prison. It advocates a social and economic system that eliminates all of the problems that have brought us upheaval in epidemic proportions, and it can redeem any individual. But if all the citizens of America became righteous, it still wouldn't be sufficient, because without the removal of the antihuman, blood sucking vampires who rule this country and the world, who continue to suck the blood of the people, we are all doomed! If we are to become a truly civilized nation, our elected leaders must be adaptable to the needs and desires of the people of all the people.

I now understand clearly why building more brutal prisons and putting people in them will not stop most of them from remaining criminals; giving them a decent chance in life, will, giving them the power to control and improve their lives, will. 44% of young African men cannot even find work in the richest country in the world, and some of us are still wondering why American prisons are overcrowded with African prisoners.

It took years to write this book because of my political activities and the constant transfers, but writing this book has been a sweet catharsis for me. I am at peace with myself and I am striving to become a "quintessential revolutionary" in the highest state of development. In a world full of fluster and change, I have no greater goal than) to serve humanity within the limitations of my capacity, and I am definitely willing to accept any personal sacrifice that furthers the cause. From the sequence of the type of life I've lived, this seems like a natural flow of things. Uniqueness, as I see it, is caring for others and standing up, regardless of the consequences, to make this a better world to live in. This embodies the noblest quality of a human being.

Epilogue

"All across the country new cellblocks rise. And every one of them, every brand new prison, becomes another lasting monument, concrete and ringed with deadly razor wire, to the fear and greed and political cowardice that now pervade American society."

   Eric Schlosser

I was transferred from the prison system of New Mexico to the Connecticut prison system in March of 1989. The younger prisoners here seem to be existing in throes of regressive behavior. There is no war here between the prisoners and their keepers. Most of the prisoners know the guards here from the streets of certain sections of the various Connecticut cities. Prisoners and guards joke and play with each other incessantly. Attempting to adapt to this imprudent prison environment has been a challenging experience for me. There are more inmates than convicts in all American prisons, but I've never seen it this unparalleled.

I'm older, sharper and wiser. The guards and inmates grant me my space. I've competently formulated my ideas and my commitment to these ideas since being in this state.... the benefit of this environment is that it has been easier for me to pursue the completion of my metamorphosis.

I'm still the agitator, but with the forbidding mind of the freethinker. I'm now able to make crucial decisions about my life and my contributions to the struggle without the aid of an outside authority. To open your mind and free your intellect is the only genuine freedom one can have. I'm convinced that this wisdom must be utilized to help others who're treading upon the rigorous path I once followed. I understand now that dogma is the enemy of human freedom. Years ago, I'd read this statement in Rules For Radicals, by Saul D. Alinsky, without grasping it because I was trapped in the "ritualized mentality" that stagnates most of us.

An analytical mind will reach out for the truth by exposing itself to the curiosity of every side of an issue. This is confirming intelligence that is not manipulated. This is also the only mentality that will one day free us all.

Writing and self-examination continues to be a healing salve for me, but nothing has been more solacing or stimulating since I've been in the prison system of

Connecticut than the sagacious, sovereign like women I've met or communicated with. These enchanting women touched an open wound, restrained my flaunting, made me stand at attention, and gave me the incentive to regenerate the straying faith in our ability to stay afloat in this poisonous social structure without relinquishing our dignity or humanity. A few of them are greeted by the people with great acclaim all of them merit maximum respect.

Dr. Lenora B. Fulani, a formidably, uncompromising sister was a presidential candidate twice, and was the first black woman to qualify for federal primary matching funds. She's also a developmental psychologist. She keenly enticed me into the political arena with her masterly insight of American politics.

Gwen Mandell, assistant to Dr. Lenora Fulani and my comrade in arms was a soldier in the struggle with a wholesome and down to earth character.

Professor Angela Y. Davis, a witty and courageous sister. She was acquitted of murder, kidnapping and conspiracy charges in San Jose, CA, on June 4, 1972. She's an author, lecturer, and professor at the University of

Santa Cruz. She visited me and illuminated this sunless tomb of zombies.

Roberta Goodman, a former assistant to Professor Angela Davis, who used to tolerate me and my eccentric probing of Angela's whereabouts. She is a patient and dedicated activist in the struggle.

Sister Ama, a former house keeper and helper for Professor Angela Davis, our political conversations on the phone would always improve my spirit.

Stefanie Kelly, Angela's current assistant; a warm and pensive comrade who has sent me some of the most considerate letters I've ever received.

Ramona Africa, the Minister of Communications for the MOVE organization; she was convicted and sentenced to seven years in prison for riot charges after she was severely burned in a fire caused by the police bombing of the MOVE apartment; this bombing generated the deaths of eleven MOVE members. Released from prison after serving the entire seven years, we became comrades through engaging phone conversations.

Ericka Huggings, an ex-Black Panther whose husband, Jon Huggings, a Black Panther leader, was shot down during a meeting of the Black Student Union at UCLA. The few times I talked to her on the phone, she always responded to me like family.

Michel McQueen, a gifted, straight to the point correspondent for ABC's Nightline. Her letters of fervor inspiration enhanced my focus upon the freshness of my ideas and writing.

Bonnie Kerness, the coordinator for the National Campaign to stop control unit prisons. A reliable seeker of justice for the thousands of voiceless convicts being devoured by a "slow death" in the savage control units. She has aided immensely in my endeavor of faulty research.

The evil continues. The Virginia prison system is still engaged in imperil treatment of the prisoners there. The names of the wardens and directors have changed, but the beast's appetite is still insatiable; a stigma this country per severely ignores.

There are over one million prisoners in America's prisons today. 89% of these prisoners are still black and Hispanic. More prisons are being built and being filled every year. The crime rate is not going down like these silver tongued politicians proceed to feed the people. The indifference the prisoners receives from the people stems mostly from their acceptance of the politician's steady ranting that they (prisoners) are all animals, and that they deserve to be treated as such. Also, the 13th Amendment makes the prisoner the only legal slave in the country. To many Americans, this renders it beyond reproach.

The Virginia prison system uses different terms now concerning the guards and wardens and prisons. They're called correctional officers, superintendents, and correctional institutions. This prudent strategy" is designed to diminish the harshness of these places in the minds of the people. Every new method is only there to deceive. I agree with one of Bonnie Kerness's statements: "The wall of silence that has been built around prisons and prisoners has got to be broken down."

The antiquated state prison in Richmond Va. was razed. The modern prisons being built today are usually smaller versions of hell. They're fashioned to cage the so called worst of Virginia's youthful population. Interaction between prisoner and guard is limited. Prisoners can be housed in these high security units for years. These super max prisons have become the trend. The lessons of Mecklenburg are lost in a spiral of power and cruelty.

The get tough on crime surge motivated the Virginia prison system to abolish parole, and longer prison terms are required for repeat offenders. This automatically traps prisoners and guards as quarries in a quagmire of hopelessness, hostility and ferociousness.

On December 27, 1996, at Buckingham prison, convict Dennis K. Webb, who is not eligible for parole until 2069, cut Warden Eddie L. Pearson from his lip to his ear with a prison made knife. Soon after this attack on Pearson, approximately 30 prisoners crushed through a fence at the prison and rushed toward assistant warden Henry Ponton and Major Calvin Booker. Warden Pearson signaled an armed guard inside a control room. The guard shot the dashing prisoners with an AR-15 rifle. Two prisoners were shot in the hand, one was grazed on the neck and the fourth was shot in the arm. The state's new Director Ron Angelone, as Robert Landon before him, made an absurd statement in response: "The prisoners' actions were spontaneous, did not reflect overcrowding, restrictions or external factors. Let's put the blame where it belongs, on a bunch of juvenile delinquents in adult bodies."

The war goes on. The new governor George Allen is identical to ex-governor Charles Robb. Joseph O' Dell III, who was convicted and sentenced to death for the 1985 rape and strangulation of a Virginia Beach waitress, was denied an appeal for clemency by governor Allen, in spite of pleas from Pope John Paul 11, Mother Teresa and Amnesty International. O'Dell was executed by lethal injection at 9:16 p.m.: this happened while he was being denied access to the "genetic testing" evidence that could possibly prove him innocent!

Two horrid, Mecklenburg like control units continue to show the nature of the beast: Wallens Ridge, in Stone Gap Virginia, and Red Onion, in Wise County, Virginia. Both were built in 1998. Both have also been cited for human rights abuses. Among the abuses at Red Onion cited by Human Rights Watch are: prisoners being fired at with shotguns for minor infractions; excessive and punitive use of electric shock stun devices; living conditions that are degrading; and prison guards subjecting prisoners to racist remarks, and harassing conduct.

One prisoner told the Human Rights Watch, "The day I arrived I was told that I was at Red Onion now and if I act up they would kill me and there was nothing anyone could or would do about it."

In the first nine months after Red Onion opened in August 1998 prison guards fired weapons at prisoners 63 times.

The Connecticut prison system is now sending Connecticut prisoners to Red Onion as a favor because Virginia prisons does not have enough prisoners who has evidenced dangerous conduct to fill Red Onion or Wallens Ridge.

On August 22, 1999, a guard at the newly opened super-max Red Onion state prison was stabbed about eight times while delivering lunch trays. Jackie A. McCarty was attacked by prisoner Lamont Douglas, 24, who was then shot twice with rubber pellets by a guard in a gun port.

Abdul "Cup Cake" Wakil, one of the real ones, was sentenced to life for the murder of another prisoner at the State Farm in State Farm, Virginia. He was originally doing 50 years for murder. Cup Cake has been locked up for over 20 years.

Henry "Bobilly" Gorham was transferred out of state to Kentucky in 1987. He was transferred back to Virginia six or seven months later. He also received an added 40 years for the stabbing of a guard on April 18th, 1985.

William "Rubar" Pollard was also given 40 years for the stabbing of a guard on April 18th, 1985. Rubar has been in prison now for almost 30 years.

Paul Comer was transferred out of state to Kentucky.

John "Blood" Turner is still in one of the hell holes of the Virginia prison system.

Rico "Doc" Holiday is still in the Virginia prison system. He's doing over 100 years.

Thomas "Top Cat" Pen was killed by another prisoner at Mecklenburg in 1987. He was stabbed from behind, in his style of attack, through the brain.

Malcolm "Mack" Jefferson was transferred out of state to New Jersey. He has been locked up over 30 years.

James "Sporty" Washington is still in the Virginia prison system. He has been locked up over 30 years.

Ahoto Mulazim is still doing time in the Virginia prison system. He was sentenced to 12 years for stabbing his lawyer with a prison made knife in the court room in

1985. Ahoto was not pleased with the tactics of his lawyer while he was on trial for attacking a guard at the State Farm.

All of the six death row prisoners who escaped with James and Linwood Briley have been executed. Big Lem D. Tuggle was the last one to be executed. He went to his death on December of 1996, uttering his last words with a smile, "Merry Christmas."

Willie "T" Turner was executed on May 25th, 1995. I had informed his lawyer to be sure to inspect his personal typewriter after the execution. Inside the typewriter, tucked in a cut out slot, his lawyer was staggered when he saw a blue steel .32-calibre Smith & Wesson revolver. The gun was loaded, and the typewriter concealed a plastic bag filled with bullets. A reporter by the name of Peter J. Boyer wrote a long article in the December, 1995 issue of the New Yorker magazine. It was titled "The Genius of Death Row."

I've been in prison for almost 20 years now. I've watched my confident daughter, Kim; grow into an independent and progressive young woman. She has given me love, support, and two handsome grandsons. I deem this to be a reflection of the future. The conscious youth is our only hope. I'm acutely impressed with my daughter and the advanced young adults born in the hip-hop generation. All of them are not on drugs or murdering each other. Tupac Shakur and Biggie Smalls had the power of influence, but they vacillated between commitment to the struggle and stereotyped negativity. This left their followers/fans stupefied.

When this generation is finally persuaded by young, selfless soldiers like Monifa Akinwole, leader of the community based organization Malcolm X Grassroots Movement, which has chapters in 13 cities and two prisons, our objective to change this country, change the world, will not be such a remote idea.

I can only hope that this book of dissent has done some good. I will conclude with one of my own favorite poems:

A Convict's Promise

Out of slime and lies and horror

I will bloom like a

Rose

Years of mental and physical pain,

Neglect, loneliness, isolation

Will be authentic in my

Strength and love

Will show the world that a

Tortured convict can grow

Like the caterpillar,

Into something

Beautiful